gasstationthoughts
and
the daily journal of wheeler antabanez

matt kent

Fort Lee, New Jersey

Published by Barricade Books Inc.
185 Bridge Plaza North, Suite 308-A
Fort Lee, NJ 07024
www.barricadebooks.com

Library of Congress Cataloging-in-Publication Data:
Pending as of press time. Contact the Library of
Congress for this information.

Printed in the United States of America.

10 9 8 7 6 5 4 3 2 1

editor's note
by Jeff Nordstedt
Vice President
Barricade Books

At Barricade Books we believe that there is no such thing as too much information. We have published books like *The Anarchist Cookbook* and *The Turner Diaries*. It is important to provide a forum for those whose voice is suppressed by the government, the mainstream media, or any of a slew of culprits who currently threaten the sanctity of our right to free speech, as insured by the First Amendment of the Constitution of the United States.

The premise is simple: knowledge is never as destructive as ignorance. Marginalizing a voice only forces it underground to fester. Allowing that voice to be heard opens it up to public debate.

Renegade publisher Lyle Stuart, who, as it turns out is also my boss and mentor, likes to tell the story of a friend who survived the Holocaust only because his mother got a hold of a copy of *Mein Kampf.* Upon reading it she knew it was time to move her Jewish family out of Europe. I am almost certain that the current political atmosphere would not allow for a book such as *Mein Kampf* to surface in the United States. But I am not so sure that we are better for it.

3

What you are about to read may be the most subversive book you've read. It is almost sure to draw the ire of people across the political spectrum. As a matter of fact, it already has. The author has been arrested for the words you will read in these pages. Eventually the charges were dropped, but the attempt to silence a voice of dissent should not go unnoticed.

Admittedly, this book is indicative of social problems. That can be said without debate. What can be argued, however, is the question of precisely what those problems are.

The threat of teen violence, particularly in schools, remains a sensitive issue now, nearly two years after the shootings at Columbine High. The drama surrounding this book began precisely one year after the infamous events took place in Colorado.

Matt Kent's story truly begins years before the Columbine incident. He, like so many kids today, was raised to tow the line, to fit in at all costs. Like tens of thousands of other American kids, he was raised on the mixed messages of the media, and the detached moralism of his parents, preachers and teachers. Perilously close to being overwhelmed by the pressure to become what he was not, Matt Kent found an outlet. He began to write.

I do not pretend to relate to, or for that matter agree with, his penchant for pursuing violent fantasies in his writing. But the fact that he began to look forward to working simply because it afforded him the time to write—to unburden his thoughts—is inspiring.

By arresting Matt Kent for his thoughts a message is being sent that says "suppress your violent feelings, lock them up or we will lock you up!" Locking up Matt Kent and other young people for what they think will simply drive adolescents struggling with their identity further inward.

The difference between Matt Kent, Dylan Klebold, and Eric Harris is that Matt Kent found a voice to express himself without having to resort to violence.

The words he was arrested for were those of a fictional character created as an outlet for his feelings. If we continue to silence voices like his we will only end up with more kids lashing out at a society takes the position of silencing unpopular thoughts in order to keep people in control. The result is to worsen the problem we hope to solve.

Now read this book with open eyes. Be shocked, be horrified, be amused. If you relate to the ideas in this book, I hope you find comfort in knowing that you aren't alone. If you hate the book, I hope you do so with the wisdom to see that it is just art, an expression of a mindset that can be found in High Schools across the country.

The majority of this book appears virtually unedited. It is our attempt to provide an insight into the voice of a generation. It is a voice that is undistilled by media pundits or reactionary politicians looking to blame rock music, violent video games or whatever the culprit of the week may be. It is a voice which must not be suppressed.

DEDICATION

these words are dedicated to the youth of america
who with my help shall conquer the world

"I'll make a final explanation and this one will be really final. My father is a businessman trying to provide for his wife and children and those friends he might need someday in a time of trouble. He doesn't accept the rules of the society we live in because those rules would have condemned him to live a life not suitable to a man like himself, a man of extraordinary force and character. What you have to understand is that he considers himself the equal of all those great men like Presidents and Prime Ministers and Supreme Court Justices and Governors of the States. He refuses to accept their will over his own. He refuses to live by rules set by others, rules which condemn him to a defeated life. But his ultimate aim is to enter that society with a certain power since society doesn't really protect its members who do not have their own individual power. In the meantime he operates on a code of ethics he considers far superior to the legal structures of society."

—Michael Corleone
The Godfather

begin here...

we live in a fucked up world. a world consumed in consumption. violence our foremost form of communication. technology mutated into a disease of convenience. persecuted for our petty addictions. how much longer do you think this is gonna last this world of religious wars and retarded politicians? our whole existence is about to go up in flames. nuclear winter is fast becoming our only option. we have used technology for insane purposes. we build zillion dollar armies and waste our time on borders and politics instead of simply having fun together. the inevitable destruction of the human race is the ultimate irony of our nature. we fuel ourselves with lies. our story will end the same as all our other stories, tragedy. star crossed lovers all of you. this time it will be me nailed to the cross.

humans love to cry. we are the only animal that can do it so we might as well take advantage. we thrive on the drama of our lives like a plant drinks in the sun. our friends and family lap up our tears to replenish their own wells. we pretend to hate violence but every last one of us has restless hatred festering on the inside. soon we will see WWIII. the signs are all around us. the writing's on the wall.

so what does a guy like me do in the midst of all this chaos? try to form a routine? try and sedate myself into believing everything is going to work out in the end? i have lost the ability and the inclination to lie to myself.

introduction

i am a man who refuses to pretend. a man who can no longer waste his time working a job. a man put to sleep by the drama of this world. for the last four years i have been laying the foundation for my own world. a world constructed from the ideology of my own morality. far too consumed with my own life to care about humanity's fate, i refuse to bend to the rules that make this world comfortable. instead of joining the flock and accepting the lies around me i work to spark the change that will burn those rules at the stake. i declare myself the main character. i write, i make web sites, i turn my life into entertainment for you. all my words are just one long suicide note. i am the man who will touch off the final inferno, the man behind the end.

writing is my weapon. each sentence a full metal jacket. there are lots of people in this world that want to tell me what to do and i hate them for it. i follow my own dreams no matter what the odds. sure, i've failed in the past, found myself trapped in various embarrassing dogmas, but through it all i have always made it a point to learn from my mistakes. i have taken all i've learned and invented my own goals. i separated the good advice from the bad and found my own morality. i studied the world for 23 years and then threw everything they taught me back in their faces. i have turned my words into a one way ticket to freedom, but lately the fare for that ticket has been growing exorbitantly high.

recently my words have been the source of some considerable controversy. it seems the masses of people do not like to be swayed from their routine. they do not want to invest time in thought. they would rather curl up in front of their tv's with a glass of wine and pretend the world has a laugh track. they want to go to their jobs and make lots of money so they can live comfortably. so many people in this world are living so very comfortably. they follow all the rules, believe all the lies, and spend and save this world into a cozy place to live. my world is not so very comfortable.

my world stands naked to the public. i opened my door and ran out to meet you. i did this because this world is a joke and i wanted to let you in on it. no matter how important you think your life is you are nothing more than a tick of the clock. our time here is short and pointless. our efforts at greatness are hopeless because we are nothing more than tiny little mites inhabiting a speck of dust in space. in a universe so unimaginably vast it's ridiculous to believe that a life could actually mean something or make even the smallest impact. your life is a brief and common gift that will never mean as much to other people as it does to you. it is in this obvious truth that i have found my freedom. i realized that the only person who really cares about my life is me so i had better start doing something that i enjoy.

i know what you're thinking. you're thinking that there are plenty of people who care about you and there is no way that your life doesn't affect them, but my friends you are missing the point. your loved ones are just as inconsequential as you. the only reason they spend their time loving you is because it benefits them in some way. they love you for their own reasons and they keep you around because it makes them feel good. i see life as a precious gift, but never under any circumstances do i pretend that it means anything. i am not so insecure that i need to lie to myself about my purpose on this earth or my inevitable mortality.

the first time the pointlessness of my existence sunk in was my first taste of pure freedom. all of a sudden i was free to make mistakes, free to invent my own rules, free to risk, free to love, and most importantly free from fear. no matter what i do and no matter how hard i try i know my actions will never mean a goddamn thing so i'm just going to have as much fun as possible before i die.

my brand of morality is not accepted by our comfortable little society. speaking my mind is all i have to do to get myself in trouble, and i know that if i'm in trouble i must be doing something right. i feel the cops breathing down my neck wherever i go, relentlessly surrounding me. because of my nature i have always had small skirmishes with the law but it wasn't until i transformed my life into a public spectacle that they decided i was a real danger. the trouble started when i posted *gasstationthoughts* on my web site: welcometohell.net.

i created welcometohell just for fun. it began as a digital tour guide to a complex of abandoned hospital buildings near my home. originally the hospital served as the last resting stop for thousands of hopeless tuberculosis victims but now the few buildings that remain are themselves decaying corpses. i grew up in the shadows of this immense structure, smashing sinks and toilets with a sledgehammer, spray painting, getting fucked up, breaking windows, lighting fires, studying anarchy from the inside, and learning what true freedom is all about. when i finally got a decent computer i noticed that no one had ever made a web site about my favorite place so i decided to make one myself.

the site contained pictures of the buildings, a history of the hospital, and all the other shit that i thought was fascinating. once the site was up and running i spray painted welcometohell.net all over the walls and the roof of the hospital. all the local kids who hung out there saw it and word quickly spread across the internet about my web site. to make things interesting i added a series of

14

unmarked hyperlinks that served as a window into the mind of my best friend and alter ego wheeler antabanez. most of the hidden hyperlinks led to little bits of wheeler's writing and one of them pointed to the book which you are about to read. i had written *gasstationthoughts* when i was nineteen while working the late shift at a local gas station. it began late one night during a snowstorm with one sentence scrawled on the back of an amoco earnings report: "soon a car will pull up spitting and blowing and i will once again be overcome by the cold." that's all it took to get me started and before i knew it i was addicted. i couldn't wait to get to work everyday to write. i found an old notebook lying around and i began to fill page after page with my thoughts.

gasstationthoughts was my first real introduction to wheeler antabanez and the first of many projects designed to liberate myself from the hopeless world of a high school drop out. at first he just read over my shoulder and whispered into my ear, but as i became more engrossed in my writing i actually felt him invading my body. by the end of the book, there was no separation between the two of us. i was just a half of someone else. wheeler was not content living in the dead end world that matt kent had created for himself. his ambitions were higher and, although he would have to wait several years before he really came to power, his influence began to amplify my personality and change the man who i was to become.

as word spread about welcometohell.net more and more people began sending me their reactions to *gasstationthoughts* i was shocked at how much they seemed to enjoy reading it. shortly after i posted it i began receiving hundreds of e-mails asking me to exhibit more of my writing. this was the first time i had ever let people read my words and i was over-whelmed by the praise wheeler was getting. there was no choice, but to give the people what they wanted. wheeler responded by starting an on-line daily journal where he began to openly explore his newfound consciousness. the journal was the per-fect platform for reaching massive amounts of peo-ple and with the encouragement from our audience wheeler's voice steadily grew into a cathartic rave directed at anyone who would listen.

and they did listen. the people around me wanted more. they were intrigued. once it had begun there was no stopping the momentum. people all over new jersey knew about my site. i advertised in a popular underground magazine called weird nj and my e-mail box was always full. kids wrote me long e-mails asking me my opinions about shit that mat-tered to them; stuff like music, sex, and columbine high school. the whole thing was just a little glimpse of the rock star life and it was downright intoxicat-ing. once i had a taste i was hooked so i developed a plan. i put the razor in the hand of the killer and said "take this and do whatever you want." wheeler spoke his heart out and nearly killed us both.

the events that followed wheeler's liberation into unrestrained words were nothing short of madness. his words were a reflection of the chaos that has been the theme of my life. for years i have struggled to find my own way through this merciless existence. all my life i have been molded to play the role of the mediocre white suburbanite. it wasn't until wheeler had fully surfaced that i was finally able to break free and cry out in a voice of my own. once people caught on all i could do was sit back and enjoy the ride. i learned long ago that when wheeler has an idea in his head nothing can stop him. he pushed it as far as he could ranting, promoting, going crazy for the whole world to see. the whole thing was like a backward political campaign, his motto: "don't vote for me i'm an asshole." but then on april 19th the day before the one-year anniversary of the columbine high school massacre the cops showed up and tried to put an end to that campaign.

i will not pretend that i didn't know they were coming. the pigs were a key component to the plan. i fully understood wheeler's vision and i knew that i would have to sacrifice my freedom in the present for absolute freedom in the end. so when they did arrive i was waiting for them, strategically positioned on the roof of the building across the street from my apartment. my daughter was safe at her mother's house and i was waiting to rendezvous with my new girlfriend. the clock had just struck 10:00 pm. she arrived right on time. as i watched

introduction

her car disappear into the parking lot behind my building i observed an unmarked police car pull into the parking spot next to my driveway. three plain-clothes cops wearing squawky radios and 9mm's strapped to their hips stepped from the car and quickly moved to intercept my girlfriend. she came in from the backdoor to the main hallway of the apartment just as they slid in through the front. meanwhile i scurried down the fire escape, sprinted across the street and followed the cops through the front door of my house. this was the day i had been waiting for, the day that would decide my future.

as i burst through the door relief spread across my girlfriend's face and the head cop wasted no time in asking, "mr. kent may we have a word with you?"

and then it began. good cop bad cop all night long just like in the movies. they wanted to know every-thing about my life and they wanted to see every nook and cranny of my apartment. being the gen-tleman that i am, i decided to open up my home and let these intruders in. i thought i had my bases cov-ered. to the best of my knowledge all the drugs in my possession were safely concealed, but unfortu-nately during the search one of the detectives found a roach sitting on my dresser. the roach was in plain view, clipped up, ready to go, and i was fucked. the cop told me that if i had anything else now would be the time to show him. i made an on the spot deci-sion to cooperate and handed over the rest of my stash which consisted of two joints and some para-

18

phernalia. the last thing i wanted were a pack of k-9's sniffing around my backyard so i satisfied them with the little bust.

but the little bust was not to be the only bust on the schedule that night. what the cops really wanted was for me to write a retraction to all the things i had posted on the internet. this was obviously an impossibility, but at this point i have to admit that i was getting a little nervous. with the three cops watching me, i switched on my computer and brought wheeler's daily journal up on the screen. "what the fuck am i supposed to write?" i asked

"look matt we respect your creativity and we would never want to make you write something that you don't want to write. you can do it your own way in your own words, but we want people's minds to be put at ease. you have a whole town of parent's out there who are scared stiff to send their kids to school tomorrow and its because of what you have been writing in your daily journal. the phones to both police stations in caldwell and west caldwell are tied up with concerned parents and only you have the power to remedy the situation."

i looked up at him and said, "it wasn't what was written in the journal that has you here it's the rumors that these stupid fucking kids started about me. i never said anything about shooting up the high school and i don't see why anything that i said should be retracted in any way."

19

that's when they started to get a little pissed, and their anger made me think twice about the seriousness of the situation. this was full force fascism carrying guns in my bedroom and i didn't know what the fuck they were going to do to me. i sat there weighing my options and swiveled my chair back to the computer. i pulled the keyboard out of its drawer with shaking hands and the three cops pulled in close for a better view. i sat, they stood, all four of us glued to the screen. my mind raced to think of something to write that would clear this whole thing up, but as i watched their reflections in my monitor something snapped inside me. it was the same thing that always snaps when i sit down in front of this machine. i felt matt kent die and wheeler antabanez step into full character. my hands stopped trembling and my mind suddenly became clear. fearlessly, i began to type, but they only let me get out one sentence before they took me to jail. here is what i wrote:

> "the day i found out that eric harris and dylan klebold walked into school and murdered their fellow classmates my life changed forever."

i had barely typed the "r" in forever when they radioed in to headquarters and told them they were bringing me in. i switched my computer off without even shutting it down properly and was immediately slapped into handcuffs. my girlfriend started to cry, the lights began to flash, and within three minutes i was stripped of my belongings and placed behind bars. i had learned from past experience that yelling and screaming wouldn't help with the cops so i just sat on the hard wooden bench and thought about my life.

i thought about everything wheeler and i were trying to accomplish in the world and i smiled to myself as i realized what a great story this was going to make. i thought about my daughter lying safe in her mother's house. i thought about my parents who have long since been ashamed of me. i thought about *gasstationthoughts* and how much i loved it and wanted people to read it. i thought about all my loyal fans and how proud they would be that i didn't sell out to the pigs. i thought about the line "this is the first day of my last days" and i knew that on this day it was true.

on april 20, 2000, the one-year anniversary of the columbine high school massacre, i walked out of the caldwell police station feeling like a fucking rock star. thousands of people were reading my writing, my words were finally on the table for everyone to enjoy. from my perspective this was my finest hour. unfortunately my parents and everyone else in my life did not share the same enthusiasm. i tried to explain to them that it was actually a great thing because i would fight the charges in court and do my part to help keep the internet free. i told them that now i would be able to publish my book and the whole world would read my thoughts. i told them that now i will be able to live out my dreams and soon money wouldn't be a problem for me because i was finally on the right track.

but they didn't buy it. all they could talk about were the articles in the paper and their name being dragged through the mud. all they could see was the $5,000 they had just wasted on bailing me out of jail. there was just no talking to these people so i walked back to my apartment rolled a joint from a hidden supply and wrote the last journal entry to welcometohell.net.

the fucking heat was cranking all summer. from april to june i played the waiting game with the courts. months felt like years as i tried in vain to live my life peacefully. the cops were always hovering. the local kids kept coming to my house trying to meet me, and the death threats arrived as frequently as my fan mail. i was constantly plagued with prank phone calls. the mother of my daughter revoked my half of the custody so i was forced to watch her at my parent's house under close supervision. the bill collectors began knocking on my door and, one by one, my utilities were turned off. the only thing that kept me going was wheeler's plan for the future. wheeler demanded that i use the media attention that my arrest supplied me to my advantage. he dragged me out of bed every morning forcing me to work on welcometohell's sister site jesus666.com. he nagged me to stop being lazy and start looking for a publishing company. he took the initiative and turned my life around.

the search for the right publishing company did not take long. after several of my submissions were quickly rejected i realized that i had to try something different. i called up a bookstore and asked the girl behind the counter who published the anarchist's cookbook. she told me it was barricade books and as soon as i saw their web site i knew *gasstationthoughts* had found a home. it took three months of repeatedly explaining wheeler's plan to convince them that i wasn't just some maniac off the street, but when they finally signed my book they backed me 100%.

then it happened, three months after my arrest, just as my deal was being finalized, i received notice to appear in new jersey state superior court to answer to the charges of terroristic threats. i showed up in court for the first time armed with reporters and ready to fight without the benefit of legal counsel. the whole foundation of my case was that all the writing and web design were the work of a fictitious character named wheeler antabanez and were never intended as anything more than art. i also wanted to make them understand that my work is nothing less than art and is not subject to change by any authority but my own. i was fully prepared to shove the first amendment right down their throats. unfortunately they weren't as stupid as they seemed. the judge understood my case just as well as i did and he knew that it would be impossible to convict me. he also knew that the whole thing was probably one huge publicity stunt on my part and he wasn't about to send the message to the american kids that it's ok to manipulate the system for personal gain. he understood my tactics so he asked me to take a voluntary psychiatric evaluation, which i accepted, and he asked me to "tone down" my writings on jesus666.com, which i declined.

the suppression of my case was evident from the very beginning and i spoke about it candidly on the site. for the first time in my life i came face to face with the dreary, boring, details of the american legal system and i couldn't help but complain about it. you can smell the incompetence as soon as you walk through the courthouse door. newark, new jersey, one thousand paper pushing municipal monkeys armed to the teeth and ready to ruin my life. these boys weren't kidding around. their court is nothing but a fortress of justice gone corporation, the war zone's command post. once you enter those doors you might not ever leave. i made 8 official trips to this enemy stronghold, i went through a psychiatric evaluation for these assholes, they tried to drain my soul and squelch my voice but i had already won. i had lived true to my words and that's all that really mattered to me in the first place.

their court of law means nothing to me. the legal system will always be just a pawn in my plan. i knew from the night of my arrest that i would never do time for my sins so i never had any fear. you can judge for yourself whether or not wheeler's words are a crime. i have included them in this book so you can see the whole picture. regardless of how you decide to perceive my writing, the moral of the story is that i played my hand in life and won. i knew what i wanted and i figured out how to get it. i understood the hardships that i would have to endure, but i set fear aside and followed my dreams.

on october 19, 2000 exactly 6 months from the day i was arrested i received official notice from the courts that my charges for terroristic threats had been dropped. my name was officially cleared but i felt no happiness. i reflected back on the past nine months of my life. it seemed i had sacrificed every-thing just to publish *gasstationthoughts* and i still had nothing tangible to show for it. i was still poor, i still couldn't support my family, i had no apartment of my own and i was forced to live apart from my baby. drugs and sex had become the predominant theme in my life and everything i had left inside me was being sucked into the black hole of my girl-friend. we lived in hoboken nj, which is right across the river from weed, and just across the highway from cocaine. every night i went to sleep in a haze of shit and i knew that if i was going to write this introduction to my book i was going to have to get my head clear. so i left. i packed my bags at two in the morning and just fucking left. i had no home so i relied on an ex-girlfriend or two for some tempo-rary shelter and the charity of my loving parents to help me back on my feet.

with their help i managed to obtain a quiet apartment and set to work on the very words you're reading now. none of this has been easy. the path i have chosen in life has caused an incredible gap to form between myself and those people that choose to love me. they do not have the experience or the vision to understand what it is like to be obsessed with a dream. i fear i may have treated them harshly but it's only because they all wanted to change me. they wanted me to be joe shmoe average motherfucker and not embarrass the family, but i had my own ambitions and my own ideas about the ways success could be achieved. i have tried to explain myself a million times but unfortunately to no avail. so here i am alone with only my convictions and my dreams to keep me warm at night. but i'm in charge of my own future. i will govern my own fate. i will take this life that i have been granted and live it true to my nature. i am my own main character. all the world's a stage and this show has just begun. so sit back and enjoy boys and girls i still have a few tricks up my sleeve. things can only get worse from here so i'm gonna make the best of it.

if you ever want to find me just switch on your computer. my projects will always incorporate the world wide web no matter what medium i am working with. but for now as you embark on *gasstation-thoughts*, as you critique my thoughts and drool over my hypocrisies please just keep this one thing in mind. art imitates life. life imitates art. the only thing that makes life worth enduring are the fun

things along the way. these words are my amuse-
ment on this treacherous adventure. these words
are all i can afford to share with you so please take
them. love them, hate them, use them to save the
world, use them to destroy it, i don't care. this thing
you're about to read is called *gasstationthoughts*.
it's what i have to say right now and i hope you
enjoy it.

gasstationthoughts

by wheeler antabanez

soon a car will pull up spitting and blowing and once again i will be overcome by the cold. nothing can save my soul except warm technology. each night i watch you and millions like you pouring in and out of this gas station. driving your padded cell to other padded cells all over town and sometimes in different towns. it doesn't really matter what town. the padded cells are all basically the same built cheap, but to last and tough enough to ward off any diseases that might leak down into the minds of our children.

never thought this would be me. sitting in a gas station experiencing complete lyrical freedom. not worrying about chapters, plots, or themes—just writing. devoting ink to absolutely nothing but free time between cars. but actually, i am hoping someone will be interested in reading my jumbled thoughts. do you realize that i am a real person? these pages are my thoughts, nothing more. no matter where or when you read this it will always be how i wrote it, it will never change it will always be for you.

a lady just came in and i told her she reminded me of wonder woman. she asked me why and i told her it was because she was wearing a wonder woman suit and flying a plane made of glass. she was about ninety years old and had braids in her hair dyed the color of the rainbow. she told me she was a lesbian and her lover liked her to dress like superheroes. that was more than i needed to know and a little bit too much to believe. actually that never happened, but wouldn't it be funny if it did. it would certainly spice up my story. but wait, it already did spice up my story. that's the great thing about this job. i can do anything real or imagined.

i just sit here behind my boss's desk silently dreaming aloud on paper. the squeak of my ballpoint pen the only friend that i need on these long, cold winter nights. not really, i have you. so often i read books and forget myself. i guess you are not so lucky. all your problems exist. you will not be grateful for all my problems being so big compared to yours. this is a one-sided essay. you know who i am, but really i don't even know you exist. you could be pulling out of the gas station right now and you would never know that i am writing to you.

these pages are only a fragment of me separated from the body. when you finally read these words they will be nothing more than a memory to me, a snapshot frozen in time, a check in the bank. i love when people come to get gas in their big fancy pants cars only to search the glove compartment for three dollars worth of coins for our finest gas. don't they know that you don't have to buy a thirty thousand-dollar car and that regular gas is cheaper?

a man with strange bugle blowing eyes gave me a bible tract after i pumped his gas. it says on the front a, b, c it's simple to be saved. thank god it's simple because i don't like to put much effort into things. on the inside it says that salvation is simple but not cheap. they say that if salvation were only given to those who were morally worthy no one would have it. i usually tend to laugh at such nonsense but this time i think they have a point. just ask the reflecting god.

anyway, back to reality. what would you do if all of a sudden while walking down the street you walked up to yourself and shook your own hand? what would you say to meeting yourself and still existing in your own body? the thought scares me. my biggest fear is that late one night while pumping gas alone i will pull up in a car and give myself the finger.

the stream in the back of my little shanty is running over with mud. where does it come from? ever since i was a little boy and way before i was even born that stream has been quietly babbling to itself like an old man. how many other streams does it join before it impregnates the ocean with its rancid nj bacteria?

NEWS FLASH! some strange guy just came in to the station. when it turned out that we share the same name he pulled me aside and told me that he used a lit cigarette to trim all the stray hairs off his head. then he smiled, turned, walked back to his car, smelled his gas cap and confidently assured me that he had NEVER stolen anything from this gas station EVER. he then told me he was forty years old. "forty years is a long time to not steal anything from a place" he said as i quoted him.

people who are obviously insane fascinate me. maybe it's because i too have felt out of touch with reality. maybe it's because insanity is hilarious when you are looking at it from what i have come to know as reality. unfortunately reality is always changing and, as i am sure you know, it is not always easy to keep track of what the hell is going on.

we live in a world where movie critics have valid things to say. i am going to shoot a movie called cleopatra the moose. it will be only shots of the moose sleeping and eating. the only sound you will hear throughout the whole movie will be a man screaming psalms from the bible in spanish. we'll see what the critics say about that. i am almost positive the ones who speak spanish will hate it.

i'll drop a vial in the juice sit back and let the lunch room feel it.

that'll teach them about mandatory participation.

stand up

turn over the table

watch the whole room explode

don't worry about pretense

i destroy the soul

smash my teacher in his face

as i feel the drug take shape

i'll look around enjoy my rape

let the carnage take me

rules and structure burnt to the ground

screaming murder the only sound

once there was a little boy who lived all alone in a vacant lot on the outskirts of the town you live in. he was orphaned early in his childhood and since no one took him in he lived alone in the vacant lot which was nicknamed chester field. nobody knew why it was called chester field and nobody knew why the little boy, whose name is chester lived there all alone. but so it was, and so it will be until it isn't. chester, although only a young boy, is well read and has an understanding of nuclear physics that would surpass most science teachers his age. that's what growing up on the mean streets of your town does to a boy. it robs him of his childhood, yet at the same time it helps him with his schoolwork.

nothing changes only gets different. most people give advice because they want to be right. i try to practice being wrong. whenever someone pulls in and asks for directions i give them directions to where i think they should go. sometimes i send them to the police station, other times i send them to the library (especially the smart ones). one time i sent a lady who was looking for the library to the funeral home because i thought she was a little too smart for her own good. i knew all she needed was a nice dose of her own looming mortality to set her straight. the next day she came back to thank me for the good directions. she told me that she really needed that jump in perspective and i was glad to give it to her. so you see, even though i am always wrong i am usually right.

my friends have all used mass quantities of drugs, and low and behold, so have i. i was saved not by religion, but by degradation and loss. i sometimes enter a mysterious fantasy world filled with strange chemicals and psychedelic landscapes. the world exists only in the mind and when you warp your mind you warp your world. chaos. i remember as a fledgling drug addict, every one seemed so foreign to me. it seemed as if a bunch of people who i had known forever had simultaneously gone mad. i felt so bad for them. they just couldn't understand what the world was really about. they just couldn't grasp the concept of freedom of the mind. they couldn't see the fractal through the tree or the look of under-standing in the tom cat's eyes.

but with every freedom comes slavery. with every new life comes death whether it's now or later near or far. youth has no guarantee and age lacks true wisdom. people shrug and say, "if only i knew what i know now at your age." were you not listening? i live through hell every fucking day. all the people i surround myself with have turned out to be nothing but idiots. i understand love and loss. when you speak of wisdom you cannot specify what it is you know. sure you can balance your checkbook and program your new vcr, but the relationship you have with your wife is the same one your dad had with your mother and your kids are growing up to be just as worthless as you. tell the truth when you look at your son don't you see yourself part two, or maybe your father part three? you have learned nothing new. you are your parents in a new age of technology. your wisdom comes from people long dead and from the wires that run into your comfortable house with the same picture on the wall that hung in your great, great, great, great, great, great grandmother's house for 52 generations. fuck your wisdom and your knowledge.

your mistakes and triumphs have already been made by a million other mosquitoes. your 53 years means about as much to this world as one second worth of work while i'm getting paid six dollars an hour. wait til you see what i do motherfucker! my advice to aspiring humans would be: throw reality out the window. in reality, nothing impractical can be accomplished. however, when you create your own reality inside this reality that everyone thinks is real, you can do anything. there is never a shortage of opportunity—only the illusion of a shortage. there is actually never even really any opportunities only the illusions of them. you decide. the question i always ask myself is, should i live from what i learned in my past exposure to life or should i create my own reality? the answer is, of course, both. read this and tell me you have learned more than me. there is nothing to learn. all this is useless anyhow. let's see you balance a checkbook when you're dead. let's see you read this when the eyes in your head are only dust. let's see me do the same. it all comes back to equality. black is no better than white and vice versa. the two need each other to exist, yet they destroy each other as all colors do when mixed. they blend and seep into each other and hint at colors nobody has ever seen before and in the end it's always the same old gray.

i have been playing cruel little mind games with you the whole time. they are so complex and stupid that you probably don't even know that i'm doing it. there are so many thoughts that i have left out of this diatribe, but at the end of my pen all that really matters is that you understand precisely how i feel. i am the teachers pet with feline AIDS, a parent's nightmare come to life. obscenities will fly off my pen and into your children's eyes and they will seethe with adrenaline with my words in their heads. the right people will read this and they will know that yes there is someone who understands.

finally there is someone with a little substance. but my substance is poison. an infection.

one christmas i was at midnight mass with my parents while tripping on six or seven hits of mescaline. i sat in church watching jesus melt off the cross. the body had a nice texture that night and the blood was delicious. terrific again peter. why oh why do i do this?

i intercepted a census taker one day, on his way home from work. i kept him talking while i painstakingly lifted the mats from inside his car. this task was not an easy one and, of course, it was foiled in the end.

silence in my head. taking the scenic route tonight. after the last page is read, please don't forgive me for my words. i need to be justified by your hatred for me. feeling sorry for me is a cop out on your part. just another lie. if anything, let me inspire you to cry out into the world with a voice of your own. from now on you will always take a piece of me with you. we may never meet, but you will have known me. when you're done with the book please don't forget me. let me linger around and haunt your thoughts. let your mouth water at how it felt to have me between your ears.

sitting at this gas station for nine hours every day would have been pointless without these words. my thoughts have erupted out of me and now they are yours. all the hopes and dreams that i had before this little scheme were just first drafts of the final copy. i had to wait for the right idea to come to me and this gas station has been my catalyst, the perfect contrast to my future life. if you are reading this sentence right now, i have won.

christmas has now come and gone and the new years eve count down has begun. i have to work until midnight and i am listening to the sounds of times square on the radio. what a way to bring in the new year (1997). january 31 is my birthday and i will be twenty. no more teenage excuses and no more 1 in front of my 9 (in fact, ten more years till another 9). and to you the lady who cries every january 31st, thank you. even on these rainy nights things are still good. may the majestic beauty of the hippopotamus live forever in your mind. anyone want to pet my cat?

the hunter apologized silently to the dead deer and struggled to choke back a tear. he didn't really want to go hunting, but his boss brought him on the trip. you know you're on his good side if he invites you up to his cabin in the woods. the hunter had never killed anything before. he just wanted to be successful. he looked into the eyes of his victim and saw his own reflection. he thought to himself, "well, look on the bright side, i'll probably get a raise."

tonight i am sick with some smoking related disease. i have taken cold medication and despite the non-drowsy label on the box i'm feeling very spacey. the people i meet here in the gashouse seem to be talking to me from behind partitions of glass. their voices bob up and down like a bottle in the sea. i wonder if they notice how spooky i seem tonight? things are not cohesive around me and i think they can tell by the smile in my eyes and the frown on my face, that things will never be the same. really i long for the pleasures of sleep.

my paranoid boss is infecting me with the fear of a lunatic salesman. he has informed me that we will be observed by the "inspectors" that will be critiquing my window washing performance. "mott mott you must wash every window!" every window? it's raining you idiot. i refuse to wash windows in the rain. the boss has turned out to be nothing more than a penny-pinching customer. oh what fun it is to write a ton of pages. when the book is finished and all typed i am going to burn the notebook. that will be the best part of the whole thing. the real end.

one time i awoke with the name wheeler antabanez on my lips and now i am no longer searching for the man behind the name. imagine you had a dream that changed your life so drastically that it actually ended it.

this is my life.

gas has runneth over and has baptized my boots. i shaved my head on the coldest day of the year and now my wool gas station hat sticks to my scalp like velcro. if it were up to me i would rename everything chicken. that would be the only word on the planet.

we would all be able to understand it because each separate noun, verb, adjective, etc...etc... would have its own tone and pitch and we would use inflection and body language to communicate. for instance: chicken chicken chicken chicken, "chicken chicken chicken chicken chicken chicken."

if i was in the woods tonight deer would flock to me by the thousands. i am covered with salt from the sides of cars (washing windows). the roads are sheets of ice and my ass is soaked from slipping into an oily puddle with five hours left on my time sheet. this sucks.

if you're a pilot you gotta watch out for them peace doves. why i heard just the other day that one of those big military jets crashed because a dove hit the windshield and killed the pilot. call me goat kent.

try to picture a color you have never seen, or some-one's face that you have never met. you know just as well as i do that if i grew up on cable tv i would be writing something totally different right now (probably more informed). what is the point of all this writing, or movies, or talking, or communication in general? nothing. so why do it you ask? just because. it's like eating or drinking. same basic function day in and day out. if a baby was left alone in a room from the second it was born until the time it died how long do you think it would take? would it need to eat in order to survive? would it need the comfort of a motherly nipple? you say of course and i would have to agree.

when something completely original happens most people don't understand it. everything must pass tests before it is accepted. the bottom line for all information is that it has to be approved by every-one and anything that happens to be inconvenient gets tossed into the file marked impossible, "you a famous writer?" meeting new people is like washing your hands in gasoline, they may look clean, but they reek of chemicals and you better not go near an open flame. the truth hurts and unfortunately it's peter keatings all around.

i love fire. i wish i could wear it like clothing. i have spoken with flames, even cursed them when they threatened to engulf me. the molecules that i breathe were once flames. they have passed in and out of me forever and there was probably a time that a piece of you and i have commingled in some cave on some moon of some planet three billion years ago. it doesn't bother me that we are made up of the same material. on cold winter nights like these, it eases my loneliness to think that we were once together, at least in some way.

what if there are one or two bits of information that, if discovered, would change our understanding of physics completely? what if all of a sudden someone discovered that everything we know to be fact was based on some hideous miscalculation? maybe mother nature has a slip of paper tucked in her garter belt with the answers to questions we haven't even thought to ask. what if i pulled into the gas station right now and saw myself writing. would i collapse?

balloon balloon

up in the sky

go away

i cannot fly

make me want to go up high

but i can't or i might die

balloon balloon

up in the sky

go away

i cannot fly

make me want to go up high

but i can't or i might die

i just woke from a strange dream about the gas station (almost late). in the dream, two old people pulled up in a huge, beat-up car. in the back was a big, fat slob of a man. the two old people in the front were frantically screaming, and they somehow convinced me to get in the car so i could drive the fat man to a street in my town which i had never heard of.

when i got in and started driving i noticed that the club was still on the steering wheel and as i approached the first stoplight (red), i realized that the brakes didn't work. fear gripped me. in a panic, i looked into my rearview and saw a cop ready to run me down and take me to jail. i tried to pull the emergency brake, but the big whale just kept chugging through the intersection. as i went through, the cop's lights went on and the old couples screaming and nagging began to climax.

even with all that commotion going on the fat man in the back seat did not say a word, he just bobbed and swayed with the movement of the car. the sirens rang in my ears and the lights of the squad cars (now three) intruded into my brain. but the fat man just sat there his enormous folds rippling like jello. smash. we plow through mail boxes and then into a wall. finally, we are stopped. i look to my right and see the old couple staring to their left. i followed their eyes to the fat man whose head had become wedged between the two front seats with the force of the crash. the interior light was on, and i noticed rips on the back of the fat man's neck, but no blood only a sick ooze slowly seeping down between the seats. i looked up at the old people and saw guilt stamped in their eyes. they had killed the fat man. the fat man had been dead for some time.

my attention was diverted away from the elderly murderers as the cops swarmed our car. i watched them all in slow motion coming towards me, with screams written across their faces (no sound). then at the last second just as they were about to engulf the car they turned left like a school of fish and surrounded a house across the street. the cops were everywhere, but they weren't after the old couple or me. the head policeman started yelling into a megaphone and the whole troop of officers began to empty their guns into the house.

the instant they began to fire, my perspective shifted. all of a sudden i was inside the house. bullets and debris were flying everywhere. i needed a place to hide. i turned a corner that led into a long hallway, and at the end i saw the fat man. his body was being torn to pieces by bullets but he did not fall and he did not bleed. splotches of his coagulated insides were caked all over the walls and carpet. i began to run. SLOWLY.

then all of a sudden i was on the front porch and the firing had stopped. i stared into the flashing lights and on some new impulse i attacked them. the pigs seemed to be frozen in place while i moved at impossible speeds. i zipped around them chuckling into their helpless ears, whispering unspeakable obscenities and masturbating into the barrels of their smoking guns.

then just when i am having fun, i find myself dressed in a tuxedo at a dinner party. this guy who i didn't recognize but knew to be a long time business associate (somehow tied in with the mob) was trying to convince me to step outside with him to talk finances. i had a bad feeling about following

44

him, but i ended up going anyhow. outside it was a bright, beautiful, sunny day and i remember marveling at the birds singing in the trees. we walked for some time without speaking and as we turned a corner my associate turned and shot me in the head. i died. but, even though i was dead, i still had all my senses. to the consternation of my killer i stood up and began flailing wildly around the street with blood and brains splurting in every direction. children with parents, motorists and pedestrians all began to scream at me "lie down you're dead!" ALARM CLOCK. i return to the safety of my bed, but even now their voices are ringing in my head. i love to dream about work.

tonight on this long lonely stretch, my mind doesn't feel like letting it's thoughts be known. if there was a god watching over me tonight i am sure it would empathize with how i feel. tonight, i feel the eternity of my own soul. i can feel how the years have molded the boy/man behind this purple pen. how many times has my soul looked out of a different set of eyes? how many lifetimes have we spent together? where are you in this one. i'm right here, constructing page after page of nonsense. nonsense is always a cry for help. if i spoke like i think no one would have a clue what the fuck i was talking about (as you already know from reading this). putting thoughts on paper no matter how random they may be seems to be the theme of this never ending tirade. one long rant broken in style from day to day, night to night, car to car.

now i'm going to tell a story. there once was a boy named charlie. he started out just fine, born to two loving parents in a small town near yours. charlie was one of the cutest babies to ever exist and as he grew up he was graced with smashing good looks. when he was about ten, his parents began to get a little concerned. although he seemed normal in every other way, he had very poor social skills and had absolutely no friends. you make up the rest.

nothing seems to work tonight in the great formula of happiness. not that every possibility has been tried. happiness is up to the interpreter. it doesn't matter what the potion is made up of. some like sex, some prefer drugs, others get off on a home cooked meal with the family. my personal preference is to smoke a big, fat joint, get laid, skip the meal and smoke a cigarette. fuck your god moderation-i want it all.

it would be nice to climb a tree with a book on a nice fall day. i picture the tree to be ripened by autumn into a million shades of golden stars. people would never look up to see the strange, tattooed boy read-ing in the tree. they would pass without noticing and in turn go unnoticed. people go by unnoticed so often. they just mesh together like the cinderblocks in your basement. each block is just as important as the next, but they are all the same and they all basi-cally perform the same function equally well. the real question is not how important the cinderblock is but how important is the house? the answer: not very important at all unless it's your house. who wouldn't sell their soul for humanity, but in turn hates most of the people that surround them.

oh well, if everyone trotted around with lampshades on their heads it wouldn't be weird. people would scream and yell, "look at that guy with no lampshade on. what's wrong with him? that's disgusting!" but really in the guy's head he's thinking "why the hell are these people wearing lampshades all the time? there doesn't seem to be any specific purpose. lampshades don't feel good resting on my head, and besides, they look better on lamps." but despite his good insight he is arrested for indecent exposure and thrown in a mental institution. in order to get out he must be cured, so he becomes obsessed with having the biggest brightest lampshade so everyone will know that he is not some freak, but an honest, church going, business man.

this is your life. becoming your friends music, believing in god, getting your belly button pierced. fuck you i hope you all die. you graduate school, go to work, get married, have kids, get fat, pay taxes, go to church and do everything else that you do because some asshole got drunk and put a lampshade on his head. every time the truth doesn't fit in with reality, you crawl deeper into your pathetic lies.

the reason why you are confused is because you refuse to be honest with yourself. you can't bear to face the fact that one day you will die. or that your mother sucks your fathers dick. or a hundred other stupid things that you think might mean something. your thoughts are limited to things of a more polite nature because you wear your lampshade like you were taught. i decided to teach myself.

too much thinking and not enough exposure to the mainstream will only produce unacceptable art and a self inflicted bullet in your gut. just ask van gogh. his paintings and drawings were too strange for the mainstream to accept, but too good for them to destroy. instead they destroyed the man.

the reason for mindless sitcoms and chronically bad movies is to keep you in check. it's a trap to lock you away into the voluntary cage of mediocrity. try licking the back of the king's stamp and see if you don't get a tongue full of bitter sweet stardom. keep licking it's only a thin layer you can lick it off in no time flat. don't follow your ambition kids, it will only lead to death. get a job, buy a tv, make some kids, drink beer on the weekends, but don't smoke weed because for some reason that's much, much worse than alcohol. make sure you don't forget your two weeks paid vacation in the summer. take the kids to disney world and buy them a hotdog. oh hell, make that two with everything on it you can afford it. but no matter what kids, don't take those lampshades off your head. i don't care if it gives you an eternal headache, you must shield your eyes from what this world really looks like. flowers only look good in neat little rows and grass is only beautiful when it has been mowed. exposure to the true chaos that nature is will only leave you dirty and frostbitten probably dead. if you take the lampshade off your head you will certainly die, so keep it on please. "we love you we don't want you to get hurt. please, we didn't spend all that money on that designer lamp-shade for you to throw it all away."

enough of this.

the world works in mysterious ways. for some rea-son contemporary america wants to shut the door on reason. who cares? the stupidity of the human race lives within us all. we are nothing but a bunch of mammals shitting and fucking but for some rea-son we want to pretend we are something more. you may argue, "but wheeler, humanity's etiquette is the basis for a healthy society where we all share equal values in the eyes of the law." i agree, but at the same time i think it is also our greatest set back. morals, laws and public opinion are the three great-est motivators towards mediocrity, and even though they are necessary for society to function i want absolutely no part of any of them.

there are some things i will never forget. one of them is a girl i once loved. we only knew each other for a short time and we never even touched. whisked away by another man and probably better off that way. when i think back on our brief time together, i cringe to think at how stupid i was to not grab on to her and make her mine. every time i saw her i froze. my real personality would crawl into a hole and some

retarded asshole would step into my body. all i wanted was to kiss her, but for some reason i could not
find the courage. i was a fucking pussy. now years
later all i remember is the romance. i know it was all
in my head and she probably didn't feel it, but i did.
she was the basis of my own private fantasy world
come to life. every time i saw her i wanted her so
badly, but could not make it real. i am not quite sure
if she wanted me at all but i think she might have
given me a shot if i hadn't been so fucking out of my
mind. later in my life, i lied by convincing myself that
it was the drugs i was doing, but the truth is, she
was too beautiful. every time i went to kiss her i
would shy away because i didn't think anything so
beautiful could want me. so i live with the memory
of the feeling she gave me. kind of like a typical trag-
ical romeo and juliet story except i am the only one
who thinks so. oh well, i'm sure she is just as lonely
as me on this bitter, cold evening because after all
we are all alone.

i laugh at all the people who think they will join their
families in heaven. no matter who you are, no matter who you surround yourself with and no matter
how full your life is you will always be alone. this is
a fact. when you die you will not be taking anyone
with you no matter how hard you try. there is no
heaven and there is no hell; only death. you will not
be so lucky as to become an angel or even a ghoul.
you will become dust because you have no soul. you
were only lying to yourself all these years so you
wouldn't have to think about death.

yeah i think about death. all the time. i think about slicing my throat in the bathroom. my boss would come in tomorrow morning and find all the lights on, the door unlocked, and a horrible mess in the men's room. but not because of you G. because of me. i think of you as someone special. you were a valuable opportunity missed but you left me with a nostalgia that will never be ruined by your imperfections. in my memories you will always be beautiful and i will always love you.

soon the spring will be upon me and i will see a new life begin for the twentieth time. my future is a barren desert waiting to be filled with mistakes and disasters. i foresee pain in my future and i predict that my prediction will come true. but for now the worst pain i have to deal with is the biting cold on my shaved head.

tonight is a night of dreams. an emptiness has come along with the snow, the sound of it surrounding me. silence engulfs the frozen pumps outside while i scribble away inside my grubby cubicle. the pinky on my right hand is stained with blue pen from writing. so much writing. never before have i kept a diary. i have no experience in writing (except for a few poems and short stories). i didn't even graduate high school. the truth is i have no need for school. school is below me. i am smarter than every single teacher i ever had. i have a very good reason for hating school. when i was fifteen, my parents shipped me off to boarding school.

they classified me with a case of ADD (attention deficit disorder) all because i couldn't sit through their boring lectures and stupid explanations. fuck you! to all the psychiatrists and to all the teachers and to my misguided fucking parents i just want to let you know it was you who killed my creativity. you are the root to my hatred. you stood in my way. i was born to write and you made it into a chore you idiots. you sent me away to a school filled with retards and kids with emotional problems.

now i have figured out why. you saw something in me that could not be contained. matt kent was beginning to die and wheeler antabanez was beginning to grow inside of me. you could not understand that i could be different from you. is it such a surprise mom and dad? my mother has a virgin womb. i am the product of a teenage pregnancy, an adoption. thank god.

i am not like my parents because i am a different species. i come from somewhere else far, far away. so with a mixture of life's cruel hand and a pair of ill informed parents, my hatred came to life. most people who think they hate everyone are wrong. i have observed these so called haters and i see through their lies. most people are incapable of hate. they have not gotten past fear. they only hate a select few and they still can't admit that the one they hate the most is themselves.

my parents made a big mistake when they put me away. i lived with two and a half-hours total free time in my day, which was contaminated by the constant presence of a hundred drooling retards. a million miles from home with no one to talk to and no hopes of leaving. my weekends were even worse. i was trapped in the middle of massachusetts (my home being in nj) and there was nowhere to go. only breakfast lunch and dinner and long, boring hours in between with no drugs, no hot girls, no high school parties, no phone, no plans, no friends, no car, no life. i just want to take the time out to say fuck you to all the people responsible for inflicting this torture upon me. it makes me wish hell was real, so you could burn for ruining my childhood and turning me into a hate machine. how could you possibly be so stupid as to think this would be beneficial to me. you were all standing in my way and now alone in this gas station with nothing else to do, i am stating my case.

the people that surround me are all worthless, stupid to the core and running the world. wait until you see what i do. i will make up for lost time in between cars and make sure that i prove you all mean nothing. what's wrong? have i said too much. if you don't like the words, just put down the book. if you have been careful with it you might still be able to get your money back at the book store.

believe me i wish there were more people in the world that i liked. along the way i have found a few but most of them have been mistakes on my part. because yes, i am stupid. i have been in relationships with nothing but complete idiots. i have even fallen in love with some of them. each one leaves me more callused and cold. i don't just mean with girls, i have made bad choices with my male friendships as well. Now it has gotten to the point where I am almost completely isolated and most people have grown to despise me.

the reason most people don't like me is because i instantly notice that they are stupid and i start fucking with them. i have a weird way of doing this. usually, i start out all compliments and get really into what they are telling me, this opens them up to my attack. it is usually very subtle and i always test my limits as far as i think it's safe. if the threat of physical contact is benign i proceed to an all out verbal onslaught. i do this because i am an angry little bully.

my hatred for mankind started in the psychiatrist's chair and blossomed in boarding school. it continued to grow in rehab, and all through after care, and all through meetings up to the present. now my loathing for human beings has climaxed and i plan to kill you all with my words! i am confronted every day by the shining faces of the general populace knocking on my door for gasoline and motor oil, and they sicken me to the core. i see the pigs pulling over all the cars with black people in them and watch hordes of teenagers filing in and out of dunkin donuts all nights long and it makes me want to run away. i wish there were someone i could talk to. But all i have are my frozen thoughts pouring from my gas station hands.

tonight i am so lost in my past all i can feel is rage. voluntary blindness is not for me, i refuse to lie to myself about anything any longer. the truth is harsh but the lie is so much worse.

two halves of a broken ruler that don't add up to 12 inches. what a great idea. if i ever own my own business i am going to print my logo on a ruler that is completely inaccurate. each inch on the ruler will be 1/16 short. the funny thing is that it doesn't matter anyway. 12/16 isn't going to matter to some guy measuring margins in his office. to slip into someone's nice warm body would be very nice right now. my body is very cold.

WELCOME TO RADIO LAND! WE SELL CHILDREN! girls for $5.00 boys for $6.00 sick ones and midgets (male or female) for $3.00 and any kid over six goes half price! GET EM WHILE THEY'RE HOT! BUY NOW! kids have a thousand and one uses. you can use them to keep you warm at night, you can use them as a doorstop, you can use them to play catch with. you could even tie two together and fly them like a kite. yes you can do anything you want with them.

does your wife like to run her fingers through the hair on your back. when she was little, she never thought she would grow up to be the fuck toy of some gorilla.

the sun has set on summer and my winter is here. the cold has penetrated my mind and left me with a numb tongue. now, only my hand can convey precisely what it is that i have to say. blowing snow and sheets of ice have blanketed my emotions. i am crystallized like the drop of honey just before it touched her lips. bright brown eyes reflected in icicles as i look up at you. my complaints of cold ears and toes vanished as we kissed. melted miracles frozen at night into blobs. worms turned into ice pops beneath the cold steel ground. mosquitoes sleeping in the attic waiting for spring under warm planks and boards. hibernation into a book or a warm cup of coffee.

we have made it convenient to conquer mother nature. we win. her moonless sky shines black through the gas station window, and the silence of the falling snow insulates my shanty like a warm safe coffin. all things that have antennas are dead or hiding. the monarchs have migrated to mexico and i feel a slight touch of sadness creeping through me.

same story as you, loved and lost and then did it again. i use my women like drugs. one time a girl wrote this in a letter to me, "i love you. i don't know if anyone who has ever said that feels how i feel about you." numerous girls are now wondering, "did i write that?" these words are dedicated to all the people who ever took the time to love someone they knew they could never have. to all the people who have bought a cat knowing full well at purchase that they would love that cat and it would die. to all the people who ever took the time to love me, thank you. please remember me in your wills. please remember me just before you die. when your life flashes before your eyes, please think of me and smile.

that line in her letter struck me like nothing anyone has ever said to me before. i believed her because i knew just what she meant. to be the only one out of billions past and present who feels this certain way about another human.

i hope i don't have to die for what i believe in. i'm not even sure if i believe in anything. maybe paradise can be found in a bottle or in a poppy field. maybe it can be found in a book or a nice warm cigarette. i found paradise in a can of insect repellent one night in the mountains of wyoming, sweet relief from the deadly poison bathing my skin.

i always wanted a beautiful girl to come to my window and sing me a song. i would like it to be her favorite song. romance is such a silly joy. it only seems hokey if you have never experienced it. a lifetime of lies doesn't add up to a moment of pure bliss in the arms of a beautiful woman. that's why kingdoms fall and all stories are the same. brother will gladly kill brother for the love of a sister. vice versa too.

i have the overwhelming urge to fill five or six spackle buckets with our premium gasoline, dump them inside the gas station office and put a can of wd-40 in the microwave for a few minutes. how funny would it be to torch this fucking place. my mother would surely cry. fire has always beckoned me. it calls me now. instead i light a cigarette. not much of a compromise, but for now it will have to do.

blue blue is the color of the skies, but deep dark brown is the color of her eyes. doe a deer a female deer eyes. no my dear i do not hate you. it is my fault for forcing you to love me and trying to break you like a wild horse instead of a fragile deer. there is no way for you to love me because the me you once loved is almost dead. you and you alone have been the closest observer to the death of matt kent and the birth of his fabled replacement, wheeler antabanez. you have seen me lie to myself a thousand times and you know my hypocrisies perhaps even better than i do. it is for this reason that you will inevitably hate me. congratulations, we have once again been defeated by our past. how come your mind insists on speculating on the trivial. i remember when everything i did was a mystery to you. why have you turned into this icy wall? comfortable ruts long past being comfortable like a cold and clammy diaper that used to be warm. waves of the truth wash across our broken hearts and if looks could kill both of us would have been dead a long time ago. what will i do without you, my chica. inevitably we will have to find out. but no one knows the agonies we've suffered together. we tasted the same potential death. we let the drama pull us together and sought tragedy to justify our claims.

all night i have been holding cupped hands under an overhead heater, collecting warmth and drinking it like water. i need something to fill me up. give me a blizzard any day. it will give me an excuse to wear my favorite pair of wool socks and everyone knows you don't have to shower when it's snowing. gallivant to the summer and you'll forget to pack your favorite socks.

scare a squirrel and you will see a jumping squirrel. man can they jump. one time a squirrel hit the sidewalk from a 20-foot high telephone line and landed right in front of me (i don't think it actually jumped). it stopped me dead in my tracks and we both paused shocked and frozen in silence.

speculation between cars about theories that i have developed over the years finally has come to a conclusion. the hypothesis i have reached is that i am stupid. we all are. which is better seeing the population for what it is and hating everyone, or being blind and happy? i am really no smarter than any of you, it's just that i contradict myself openly and without fear. stupidity is the human price tag. i look around at people and all i see are retards, but the truth is i am the leader of the pack when it comes to stupid mistakes. as far as i'm concerned, the day i cash my paycheck for this book will be the day matt kent dies.

for now this is what i have to say about wheeler antabanez: the mauve dove approached me in a dream. i was sitting at the bar in this shitty dive somewhere in alphabet city. i was not yet thinking how to fund my fame. the truth is, i had not even considered fame yet.

i instantly recognized it. sweat had beaded up on it's feathers and i knew that it was nervous. it had never approached me before and the fear gripped me.

let me explain.

there have been two specters in my life. the horse bird and the mauve dove. the horse bird has frequently haunted me, from outside my window. it makes the most beautiful sound and it uses it to coax me. i followed it on many occasions but have never been able to locate it's exact position. i suspect it is watching my every move and waiting for the right moment to slaughter me.

as a child the horse bird scared me so badly that i could not bear to face the window when i slept. i felt if i slept that way, it would see it as a sign of submission on my part. i feared it would take me away and hurt me.

the second specter, the mauve dove, haunted the laundry basket that was kept in the closet under my hanging clothes. even at that young age i could tell that it was a night stalker with preternatural vision, a tracker, a keeper of records. i did not fear it as much as the horse bird at that time, so i slept facing the closet. my logic was that even if the mauve dove was able to lure me into the closet, my parent's would surely hear my screams and rescue me.

it was stealthful but sometimes i would hear it and i actually saw it on three separate occasions. the first time i saw it, it wasn't even in my laundry basket. it was in my kitchen, perched on the table. i was standing at the counter making a sandwich when all of a sudden i saw it out of the corner of my vision. it was the most majestic creature i had ever seen. rounded and curved like a melting cloud it stood poised in perfection. the shock of it brought me to my knees and my sandwich hit the floor. then in the blink of an eye, it was gone.

a few months later i cornered it in my closet. i had heard it rattling the hangers and fluttering around and upon investigation, i found it to be in the midst of a frenzy. it was grappling with some forgotten toy clown in a death match, but when it saw me it froze in a panic. THE MAUVE DOVE HAD LOST ITS COOL.

with jabs of my hand i forced it to speak. "tell me who you are." i screamed, as i poked it with my ring finger. when it spoke its voice was unexpectedly raspy. it said, "when you grow up people are going to hate you." i was so shocked by this statement that my jabs ceased for a moment and the mauve dove vanished into thin air. though i looked, i could not find it, or the toy clown it had been so eager to kill.

three years went by with no sign of the mauve dove and then one day it came back. the third time we met it was two o'clock on a friday afternoon and i was sleeping in my room, facing the closet as usual. the horse bird had gotten worse when the mauve dove left and i still viewed the closet as the only safe direction to sleep. when it first walked through the bar room door in my dream, i will admit that i wet the bed. i had time to mumble, "why in the context of a dream?" and then it was on me. i hit the floor under its mass and i felt its beak pierce my skull. it whispered into my brain, "wheeler antabanez."

rabies would be a blessing compared to what that bird gave me. a curse, a fuel, a frenzy, a disease. something snapped inside me when i heard the name. i broke down and woke thrashing in my bed. i reached up to touch my forehead and it was drenched. when i finally opened my eyes, i realized it was not blood but rather a mixture of sweat and urine. i screamed at the sun through the blinds on my window and then a very strange memory came to mind. it was of a tone that i had once heard in a friend of mine's voice. a tone so weak, and so pathetic, and so typical that it made me want to slice his fucking throat. the compulsion was real. i did not feel numb. i really wanted to kill him. i did not kill him. i don't know why i did not kill him. the compulsion was real.

that memory of pure hatred brought to life a new entity that day. i wrote down his name but i didn't need to, it is engraved in my mind and has infected my soul.

the mauve dove was never to be seen again and after about a week or so, life's cruel realities dampered the impression that the dream had left on me. from time to time i would tell the story of the wheeler antabanez dream but little did i know he was slowly incubating inside of me.

matt kent will never do anything worthwhile. he is but a host. do not mistake matt kent for a caterpillar who will one day become a butterfly. when wheeler antabanez is fully matured, matt kent will die. at the time of this essay or manifesto, if you will, matt kent is losing more and more control. he is sure to be dead within a year's time. why bother to live anyway? there is no use for matt kent. matt kent is just as useless as all the creatures that surround him

wheeler is growing out of matt kent to form a more efficient human. more than just some alter ego but instead a movie character come to life in my place. a man to play any part, a man filled with love, yet coated with evil. right now i can't tell who i am. i am torn between the present and the future and to my dismay i find myself alive every morning wishing i could just die and let wheeler take the reigns. i know it's me who's writing because of what i'll write next...KILL ME MOTHERFUCKER.

i have no time for punctuation and grammer.

already my hand cannot get even a quarter of my brainwaves on to the paper. you i'm sure are viewing it in the typed form and if you are thinking that i should have published the actual notebooks you're wrong. i am so sick of advice. if i had done that you wouldn't have been able to read it. you don't understand, i have to write fast. i am always racing to finish my thoughts before the next car pulls in and bends my mind away from the precious words flowing out of my hand. a tape recorder would certainly be nice but somehow i think it might change the mood of the whole story (what story?).

green in the mind and soft in the belly hot air and donuts and buckets of jelly. reading this fictitious documentary on my factual life binds us. even if you hate me i will love you for it because my goal is to be hated, banned and censored. i want to slap my dick across the face of humanity and laugh at their cries of disgust. the only reason this world exists is to fill the mind with useless knowledge and a fist full of pride.

i pride myself with my meaningless attributes that will fade through time just like you do. eventually, these pages will become dust and i will have truly ceased to exist. but for now i am here. i will proceed through time long after i am dead because i will leave a multi-media memorial for myself. never underestimate the power of a desperate man.

i wish satan was real. if by some chance i am wrong and satan does exist i would like to make the following offer: i will gladly sell you my soul in exchange for the fruition of my plans on earth under one condition. i want to be one of your evil minions tormenting people in my after life. i would gladly disguise my ghostly form and whisper instructions into children's ears to plant your sick seedlings in their little minds. just let me be beautiful and throw in some demonic powers so i could help you realize your lofty goals. but you're not real, you're just another lie. nothing more than santa claus gone bad.

nature is the ultimate artist so why even bother? i wish this fairy tale world that people beleive in was real. the world would be such a better place if miracles existed and angels filled the sky. but since i find it impossible to lie to myself it is therefore impossible for me to believe in god, or anything supernatural.

shimmering eyes like a tear drop waiting to fall

i can see it in her eyes, beauty beyond thought

but the rain lives inside her

wanting her to see why i love her as i cling to life

the rain still falls and drowns her

but then i remember

there is no rainbow without the rain.

once there was a boy who could no longer stand the

world. he was rather young, but he knew he had to break free. he stole some money out of his mother's sock drawer and took a walk down to the lumberyard. he ordered a delivery to be brought to his house and went home to get ready. when his wood arrived he set to work in a frenzy, building a large crate. on the sides he used a stencil to spray paint LIVE CARGO-FRAGILE-DO NOT DROP. when the box was done he used a drill to knock out a few air holes and plastered it with enough stamps to cover the postage to brazil. he put on his father's old gorilla costume in case someone happened to peak in and climbed into the box. he then sealed it from the inside and waited for the mailman to pick him up.

upon landing in brazil, his box was unloaded from the mail plane and put into a mail truck headed for the zoo. our clever hero decided this would be the perfect time for his departure so he ripped the gorilla suit off and threw on his only possessions: a pair of shorts and his favorite orange flip-flops. he then unlocked the box from the inside and released himself into the back of the mail truck.

the brazilian mailman was all the while sitting up front with blaring music completely unaware of the boy or his liberation. when they slowed to go around a curve the boy threw open the mail truck doors and made a mad jump into the woods. after tumbling through the mud he was quickly up on his feet and flip-flopping towards freedom.

he walked for three days and four nights through

thick rainforests and when he finally saw the ocean he knew he was home. his beach was unpopulated and he never saw another human again. he lived by munching on dead fish that washed up on shore and catching the occasional crab or sometimes even eating raw seagull eggs. he shed his shorts and lived naked except for his orange flip-flops. as the years rolled by he filled his time by creating a religion that involved the sea as god and his flip-flops as the messiah. the only thing he missed from his old life was ping pong and beef stew. other than that he was perfectly content. life was peaceful.

then one day while praying to the sea a large wave surprised him and knocked him head first into a rock. he lay there unconscious for hours and when he awoke he realized that his precious flip-flops were no longer securely anchored to his feet. frantically the boy scoured the beach but they were nowhere to be found. finally, it was too dark to search anymore and the boy collapsed at the edge of the ocean. he woke in the morning crying from the pain in his feet. all those hours searching for his flipflops without proper footwear had taken their toll. the sharp, brazilian rocks that lined the beach had cut deep furrows into his soles and when he tried to stand he returned to his knees in agony. HOPELESS. there was only one thing left: say goodbye to the world and join the heavens of the sea.

it took all morning to crawl up the side of the mountain whose cliffs sheltered his lonely beach. when he finally reached the top, he rested preparing himself for his final plunge. as he was about to jump he stopped to say a prayer to the sea: my sea who art on sand-aloud be thy waves-thy fishes come-thy will be done on land as it is in ocean-give me this day my daily crab and forgive me my fishing-lead me not into squalls but deliver me from sharks.

"i never thought it would end like this," he thought as he rolled himself off the cliff and plummeted into the seething ocean three hundred feet below. he hit the water like a train but somehow resurfaced and despite broken limbs managed to float. then, just before his life completely wound down, he saw them. two orange flip-flops cresting a wave mocking him with their buoyancy. through his lucid veil of death, the boy saw just how messiah-like his flip-flops really were. they took all the beating for his feet and never complained. the only sound they ever made was their reassuring flip-flopping that soothed the boy's soul. they had martyred their own life for the sake of the boy's and now they would be the only witnesses to his induction into the eternity of the sea.

the antichrist can be found in smoky bar rooms pretending to sip scotch from a glass with no ice cubes. casual contact will not reveal that he is the antichrist, but upon closer inspection his true nature is exposed. his tender eyes cast dreary shadows on the bar beneath his arms and the foreign glint of polished metal rods secretly shines from behind his teeth. the smell of christian meat causes salivation to occur. but there is salvation in that salivation because if you are eaten by that mouth the heavens feel so bad for you that it's an instant ticket to paradise.

gasoline is such a dirty vial substance. it contains cancer and its fumes promote the death of brain cells. cars seem to love the stuff. god forbid some water should seep into the tank or the engine will turn into a sputter monkey and the car won't make it home.

i'm sick of sticky fingers protruding from filthy hands. the mark of adolescence or gas station workers (in this case both). i am a masterpiece of imperfection, a salted slug at the edge of a puddle, too weak to move. i am the sulfur on an unlit match burning with potential. green beans stuck to a frying pan mushed, caked and baked. dirty spatulas covered with remains of half-cooked meals consisting of has-been ventriloquists. bathroom cleaner smells on my hands as i try in vain to rid my skin of old, oily, gas station dirt.

wishing that only my pinky were stained black from writing but instead it's my whole hand from working, and the pages are getting smeared. i need to relax into my writing like a warm pair of slippers losing myself in page after page of recorded thoughts. like a pair of scissors across the back of my neck on the hottest day of the summer, i feel a new relief behind this pen. writing is like shaving my head, sometimes i just have to unburden myself.

water-blue roses grow by the side of the path next to the gas station. llamas can be seen walking there at night. sometimes i hear their solemn hoof steps on the stones behind the fence and i know they are watching me. the llamas plan to overtake the world (of course) through coffee shops. they have invented a device that throws off hypnotic waves that will leave people with an urge for a new taste in coffee. gradually they will start a new trend. instead of using milk or cream people will start using llama urine to flavor their favorite blends. in time, milk will become obsolete, cheese and butter will all become urine based, llamas will become an important worldwide commodity, cows will be released from their thousand year enslavement and the earth will return to its natural state.

actually the earth is at its natural state. how could it not be? we have never brought anything in from outside of your god's creation. toxic waste, old dirty diapers, spray paint cans and car tires are all from this earth. when a beaver builds a dam, it changes the entire river and the ecosystem of the forest, but we don't call it unnatural. why do we continually think of ourselves as separate from everything else in this world? the universe will never catch up with our egos. whenever people talk about destroying the earth they are really talking about destroying the human race.

at the time of this writing, the earth cannot be

destroyed by man. it is more vast than our minds can imagine. when we set off our atomic bombs it merely kills things and knocks down buildings. it doesn't really destroy anything just changes the order in which they exist. all the nuclear and non nuclear weapons in the world put together couldn't destroy the earth, only the life and probably not even that. it is all as it should be. maybe if people would stop stressing over small things, like power, we would all get to live a little longer. what good is power when i'm the one in control?

the president and the pope are living sleeping, shitting, pissing, eating, machines just like a woodchuck or an antelope. so am i, and so are you. all the money in the world won't buy you immortality. no matter what angle i look at it the blood on their hands is the same blood on mine. it's easy to sit in your comfortable home and say "they" are destroying life on this planet, but the truth is we all feed off the same institutions and we all benefit from each other's crops. you drink the same soda as me, make and spend the same money as me, throw your garbage into the same dumps as me, and flush your toilets into the same river as me. i fund their programs and drop their bombs on innocent people every day of my life. i dropped the bomb on nagasaki, i built and flew the plane. if you don't understand now you never will. this joke is only funny if you know it's a joke, but the flame is still hot even if you don't know it's a flame.

by the way, for those of you who walk on hot coals: it's a trick. try taking charcoals from your grill and doing that. you'll be guaranteed to burn your feet off. the coals they walk on are some sort of weird rock that when heated glows red on the inside, but stays cool on the outside. good trick huh? if you want to be adventurous try jumping out of a plane. i jumped out and flew across the sky. when the chute opened i drifted through a cloud and when i came out on the other side i saw my silhouette in the middle of a circular rainbow. what's the point of having a fake experience?

if you have lost the magick of walking down the street then your life is pretty much over. just because you see the same thing over and over again doesn't make it any less beautiful. slam your finger in the door and you will discover that yes you do indeed have a finger. when everything works just fine we forget to appreciate it. that's why people get sentimental in jail. no one knows the sweetness of freedom better than someone in prison. who doesn't breathe a sigh of relief when they see a blind person or someone in a wheelchair? everyone has experienced loss but not everyone is grateful for what they have. but if we spent all our time being grateful we wouldn't come up with any new challenges for ourselves. i guess it only matters if you make it matter.

humans invented locks because we are greedy. the greed is piled high on both sides of any lock. i am going to invite my friends over for a gas fight. would-n't that be fun! what could be better than drenching the people you love with gasoline? i wonder how bad it hurts to burn to death. hopefully i will never have to find out. the pain would probably be so over-whelming that the body would just shut down all the feeling mechanisms. i just drew the mona lisa of happy faces. those playful eyes and that heart attack hair. how did we get to be so boring?

my hands are so dirty that they will probably never be clean again. it's not your typical dirt, it's a mix-ture of gasoline, motor oil, and engine grime. the kind of mess that stains the skin no matter how many bottles of soap i use. one more day and then oh boy three days off. this weekend i am going to the hospital. when i get there i am going to park across the street from the emergency room. just before i go in i am going to take my mini cordless circular saw out of my trunk and saw my left pinky off at the knuckle. then i am going to set the saw into the trunk along with my finger and walk into the hospital. i will tell the nurses and the doctors that i had a terrible accident with a saw and when they ask me where my finger is, i will tell them i couldn't find it. they will, of course, treat me and heal me as they have so many times before and in just a few short hours i will leave the hospital stitched, cleaned, and drugged.

when i get back home i will take my finger and throw it into a pot of boiling water. i'll simmer it until all the meat is gone, and then i will polish the bone to an ivory finish. then the finishing touches will be applied by drilling a hole through the bone and hanging it from a silver necklace. everyone will ask me what happened to my hand and instead of telling them the story i will just pull the dangling finger from out of my shirt.

and as i stood at the bank of the river the majestic beauty of the hippopotamus soothed my tortured mind. i felt free enough to rid myself of clothes. but as i did this i noticed one of the hippopotamus watching from a nearby tree. on the highest branch he sat smoking a pipe and frowning. he snickered and spat at my tiny human sized penis. he revealed what he had, a huge hippo dong that was as thick around as it was long. i hurriedly threw on my clothes and tried to scurry away, but my purple crown of water lily sounds followed me like a plague and hampered my escape. suddenly the hippopotamus were everywhere, sitting in bushes, floating like clouds, smelling like hippos and soaring like eagles.

i walk beside them now. time has passed, they have won my affection and i have bestowed upon them all my personal belongings. "never say die" is the hippo creed. "always survive" is the source of their strength. they never regret their prying observations and they always rebuke ill witted information. now we all walk in tight formation. on the jungle ride at disney world we joined hands for the grand tour, bluebirds pecking at their heads. yellow flowers are your favorite food hippopotamus and for that i love you.

i live a fairy tale of chaotic depression. each day is just as damaged as the next. no chastity for me no bonds no oaths and plenty of fun to be had. i swear i can hear them calling me all day long. pretty girls in shorts riding by the gas station on bicycles. but no it's winter and girls can't even see me through the fog on their windows or the seven layers of clothes i am wearing (still cold). but i am spoken for. wouldn't want to do anything crazy.

women are always misjudging me anyway. no one could understand what i am doing between cars until this is finished. i am examining my thoughts with a fine tooth comb while you blab to your man on your cellular phone. and the night just keeps getting lonelier and lonelier.

i love to love. sex is the needle. hugs are the drugs. your body is the pusher. why are females so much more attractive than males. i can look at another guy and see that he's attractive but only ascetically never for sex. i feel no instincts towards pro-creation but i find myself agonizing over the beauty of the female form. yeah, tom cruise is a good looking guy but i don't want to fuck him. i'd love to steal his wife away though. but gay or straight every normal human being on the planet is a pervert. there is something inherently wrong with people who deny themselves the pleasure of sex. sex is the one thing that's really fun about being a mammal and so many people try to keep it locked away. my parents were once horrified to find porno mags in my room. what could possibly be wrong with looking at pictures of truly beautiful women in the prime of their lives completely naked? my mother said that it was degrading to women and the moment she said it i knew for the first time how most women see the world. the only reason women think porn is degrading is because they are ashamed of their own bodies, their own desires, and they are jealous because they don't look as good as the women in the magazines.

it's not degrading to show off your beauty. women have been taught to believe that sex is ugly and that their natural urges were disgusting perversions. but what you didn't know is that the priest is in his room jerking off every night just like the rest of us. the only reason they make up these lies is so you will feel bad enough about yourself to need god to forgive you. think about it. the sole purpose of religion is to make you feel bad enough about being human that you will be there on sunday to drop a dollar in the collection basket. everyone who believes in god is stupid. people insult my intelligence when they try to talk to me about god. go talk to matt kent about god the only god i know is wheeler antabanez.

i wish i could find a woman who was truly beautiful and would let me give everything i have to her. i am

76

not afraid of the truth and i have no fear of my past. let my failures be known to the world. the only things that really matter are my triumphs.

tears of angels cast down upon us to tame the fires of this hell. like outcast arms, the trees reach up to embrace torrential life. doesn't this prove the tears sent down to tame the fires are really the very fuel on which it feeds? life that doesn't want life is condemned to constant sustenance. thy will be done. well, well, well you never can tell you might go to heaven or you might go to hell. out here in this cold winter, the only friend i have is myself.

today i killed a fisherman and i stole his pole

today i killed a fisherman he ain't never gonna grow old

i laughed in his face and put him in place

now i walk river road and i step on a toad

i'll use his pole for my own type of goal

i don't need it for dinner i need to get thinner

i just want to catch a big fish and kill it.

oh yes he was always different. on summer evenings all the boys would sit on the fence out in the back of old edna's barn and hoot for hours. they sounded like a pack of owls gone insane. one weekend all matt's little friends had gone off on vacations with their parents and he had no one to hoot with.

do you think that stopped him? lordy no. that boy got himself four tape recorders from god knows where and set to work all day hooting into them like a mad man. then just as the sun was setting he set all the tape players on the fence and turned them up full blast. he was joined by himself in quadruplicate. what a sight i tell you. that boy is just downright weird.

i don't feel alive, everything has turned dead inside. never asked to live this life you lead and you can't force me any longer. all i want is to be me, not brainwashed by society forced sobriety. cancel my subscription to the master plan it's now that i will take my stand and look out for my destiny to be free from everything you forced on me. all i really need is some fucking privacy.

don't call it a relapse because i never quit. i got sent to the cleaners so they could wash out my brain. it had been getting too gummy with resin and they thought they could scrape all the tar right out of my head. i laughed and said, "i'll give it a try." so i opened my mind really wide and complied. i tried it your way but coffee doesn't satisfy my needs. i'm a stoner and you know what stoners do. i am a right-handed person. why do you insist i live in your left-handed world.

pain is the only constant i have ever known. sometimes i overdose on it, but that is to be expected when you're the one filling the needle. my mind has become a sadistic masterpiece created by a relentless, unmerciful artist that you all know very, very well: YOU. you have done this to me you have made me hate you. i am by no means content with being human. i wish i could elevate myself past this horrible body. if i had one wish, it would be to become a vampire. i know they are not real, but neither are wishes.

what a nice day too bad it's wasted on sobriety. wishy washy women work well while winking. while wendy works we wink. when wendy winks we work. whales were winning wacky wizards who wore wingtips while weaving. i am a new person. the person that started this book (matt kent) has died. the front cover says wheeler antabanez and bold print never lies.

on day one, freshman year of high school (still in public school) principal jesus jackangelo calls me into his office and encouraged me to drop out. they just didn't want me there. what a way to start a new school year. now, i look back on this little power hungry monkey and laugh. i am taking what i learned in your schools and throwing it right back in your face. after reading this don't you wish i had never learned to read. teaching me how to read was like putting a razor in the hand of a killer. and yes, two years after his request i did drop out of school (boarding school).

i made my exit on a cold january night. things had been getting worse and worse at school and i was feeling extremely angry. i decided it was finally time to get myself thrown out. i took a fire extinguisher off the wall and threw it through a huge plate glass window in the boy's bathroom. the winter blew into all the shower stalls and toilets, glass was every-where and i just stood there laughing. i was prompt-ly excused forever, and on my train ride home this hot little girly smoked me up with some very tasty marijuana.

people have the dandiest things in their cars, some people offer me food. i like it when people throw me a smile for a window well washed. i don't mind doing my job well. just because i am writing this book or smoking a cigarette doesn't give me an excuse to leave cars waiting to get gas. i don't have any stu-pid ideals about my job, it's just that it's my job. that's what i get paid to do, so i do it. i don't hate my job in fact i actually like it. this job gives me time to think about things and that is really my pay-check every week.

ten and a half hours pumping gas, outside all day in the middle of december who would have thought. well my teachers maybe and certainly jesus jackan-gelo. they all knew i would be pumping gas some-day, but they had no idea i would be writing it down. what can i say formal education is just not for me. anything i want to learn is at my fingertips at any time, i just teach myself.

ever had that bad feeling that creeps through all the sunshine in your day and punches you deep in the stomach? ever realize that your soul is already sold?

every time i start to enjoy the person i have become that nagging sickness comes back. fuck it all! you're just sitting waiting for that bitch to come to earth and get nailed to a cross again. i nail myself to a cross every fucking day.

it's because of your control and your demands that i have become what i am, but i still must thank you. you have inspired me to become something better. i had you in the palm of my hand, but only long enough for me to throw you away. anger has crested in me tonight! nothing could bring me happiness on this long stretch, so i'll just come right out and say what i really feel. i just want to say to all the christians out there in this bleeding hole that i want to taste your flesh. i want to eat your pets and take your children out behind the shed and kill them. i want you all to know that i hate each and every one of you motherfuckers, and rest assured that if i achieve my goals your whole vile race of hypocritical monkeys will be erased from the planet. i have transcended your ignorance and instead of being amused i am enraged. you want me not to jerk off you piece of shit, i'll cum right in your fucking face. it amazes me that grown humans actually believe in a fairytale. i thought you were so fucking smart until you started talking about god. you insulted me by filling my little mind with ugliness and sin and capitalizing on my immaturity and lack of experience. you knew i would believe everything you told me, but you didn't know i'd grow up to be smarter than you. yeah, i'm smarter than you. you have no vision. you need to belong. you need everyone to agree with what you think. fuck you christian, jesus was a fraud. fuck you christian, i don't believe in god.

old cigarette resin and bits of food stick to my mouth and fear has seized me by the throat. nothing bad or mysterious has occurred, but despair has set in. maybe it is because of long talks with old druggy friends. too many memories brought back to life from the vaults of my mind and i wish i had a taste of something sweet right now. why do i deny myself it's like having speaker-phone phone sex or being a blind man with band-aids on his fingers. i look back with lofty disgust at my own blindness, but in the end i know i will be laughing. how can destroying one's body feel so good?

the deep end awaits me everyday. right now my edge is just about crossed and the view is nice from where i stand. for the first time i see my future laid out in front of me like a beautiful woman. it's warm and inviting and it makes me want to jump right in. all the people who have ever shared themselves with me now hate me and soon the rest of the world will join them. i want my words to hang me like a noose in front of everyone. i have no fear of death because i know that i am worthless. wheeler antabanez is the only hope for this body, so i have accepted that and given up.

do you know what it feels like to have total trust in someone and have them squash you like a bug? it doesn't feel like anything to me anymore. there is no one left to care about not even you. i could see how you might feel differently, but this is my reality. do not feel sorry for me. if i wanted to i could be your friend it's just that i would rather be alone right now with my pad and pen. i am not a hard person to get along with. if i like you and i respect you i will be kind and generous, but if you do not meet my standards i'll just throw you away.

i am one of those people who don't need other people. i spend whole days in solitude without even thinking about it. i disappear into the woods or into the abandoned sanatorium near my house and forget the outside world even exists. i don't need friends. i don't need relatives. most of all i don't want them. the last thing i need in this narrative is any outside influence from some friend. one day, when i have something more than anger to share, i will find a friend. until then, fuck you all. i am better off alone.

but listen, i also understand about love. i have loved and i want to love again, but this time i don't want to settle. i want someone who is my perfect contrast. i want someone to challenge me. i want a girl who will fuck me like she needs it, but most of all i need someone who will try to out-do me in every way and smile at my success.

so what do you think about my first book. i hoped you enjoyed it. if not, why have you read this far? are you highlighting my words as examples for why my book is to be banned from your school libraries. i bet you've got a bright fucking book by now. try keeping me off the internet motherfucker. america, you cannot save your kids from me because i am one of them. any form of information they receive from me will be exactly how i mean it. the things i have to tell them in the future will not be coded or coated in any way, they will be as this book is, a piece of me and nothing more. do not try to find me. when the time is right i will find you.

the daily journal of
wheeler antabanez

February 1, 2000

another useless day

tending my goals has become a dream

head still spinning from the night before

soulless

empty

dry

tv time

trance

sweating palms

pulsing veins

but for how long?

all this will still be here when i get back

but i won't be back

someday

my chemicals will change

my organs will fall into themselves

all my energy will be devoted to decay

February 2, 2000

even though the sun is shining through my window all the light seems to be coming from my computer screen. like hitler to a jew i'm in love with you. lately i have been frantic. running around searching for next years christmas presents. i am going to buy our new president a book on origami i am going to buy our new pope a wallet with a chain and i'm gonna buy all next years freshman AK-47s. for me the spirit of giving lasts all year long. yesterday i gave myself some more bruises. i used my hammer like an artist on my upper thighs and now they are the color of the rainbow (pictures coming soon). i was gonna take a walk to the sanatorium today but my head wouldn't allow it. i have had a lot of trouble leaving the fortress lately. maybe its because last time i left i had to come right home and clean my gun. there has been a lot of trouble around here lately. for the last three weeks the horsebird has been on my back nonstop. every night i hear it out my window and the other day i heard it in the library behind the copy machine. i haven't been able to concentrate on anything. sleeping is out of the question and my novel has fallen by the wayside. hopefully the end is near.

February 3, 2000

do you wake up and shove drugs in your face every morning like i do. ever go to work as the world is melting around you. some of us need the drugs. like a bad transmission i always find myself slipping along late for appointments, dizzy, faced and spun. wouldn't have it any other way. have a nice day boys and girls

February 4, 2000

my dreams have opened my imagination like a wound. every night a fresh gash is opened on top of old scars. last night god visited me. in the dream god crawled into bed with me and started running his fingers through my pubic hair. one thing led to another and we ended up fucking so hard that we broke the bed. god is good god is great. god had the most beautiful tits i have ever seen and an ass that sends shivers down my spine just thinking about it. hopefully tonight will bring another visit from god. maybe someday our meetings will take place in the real world for everyone to witness. until then i will keep you informed.

February 5, 2000

in an attempt to clear my head and to refocus on my projects i have decided to lay out the general theory behind my plans. to follow are some observations that i have found to be valuable lessons.

THE COLLECTIVE MIND OF THE MASS POPULATION IS WEAK.

when a mass of people is set into motion towards a specific goal it is always prompted by the will of one mind or organization. masses of like-minded people are easily programmed for a common mission.

THE STRUCTURE OF SOCIETY IS WEAK.

a society bases its laws on the shared morals of its majority. since the mind of the masses depends on the whims of the masses it is easy to manipulate society's will from the inside out.

WHAT IS THE STRUCTURE OF SOCIETY?

the structure of a society is the value systems, or morals that the masses incorporate into their laws.

HOW IS THIS STRUCTURE FORMED?

the structure of a society is shaped entirely by its media. as technology expands the capacity for shared information increases and groups of people merge into one another. the advent of technology has made society less about borders and maps and more about shared value judgments.

HOW CAN THIS STRUCTURE BE ATTACKED?

one trick to attacking a society is to prove that it's value system is invalid. for instance if you prove there is no god there will be no church. another form of attack is to use their system of beliefs for your own purpose. it is my opinion that this latter form of attack is by far the easiest and most effective. although the religious mind is weak its will is controlled by a mystic deception that cannot scientifically be proven invalid and therefore disregards the first method. it seems fairly obvious that there is no god, but despite that fact there are still billions of people across the world with strong spiritual beliefs. by adopting the opposite attitude of what the masses perceive to be right (moral) it is easy to turn a large group of people against you (especially if you are in the public eye).

WHAT ARE THE BENEFITS OF HAVING A LARGE GROUP OF PEOPLE OPPOSING YOUR BELIEF SYSTEM?

publicity is the reward for taking a stand against

a popular belief. if what you are offering is opposed strongly enough it will be news to everyone. all people will become aware of the conflict and you will have the opportunity to recruit your own mass of likeminded people (army) to use against your opponent.

WHAT CAN BE GAINED BY ATTACKING SOCIETY?

the reason for attacking a society is to change it and to hold a position of ultimate authority within the new rules. adolf hitler is the perfect example of the second technique of attack. he adopted an opposing stance to the jews and convinced a nation that he was right. it is my opinion that hitler was more interested in the attack than in his convictions. anti-semitism was a convenient avenue towards leadership because it was a pre-existing value judgement common to his people.

WHAT IS THE MOST IMPORTANT WEAPON IN A WAR AGAINST SOCIETY?

the most valuable tool in a war against a society is media that is absorbed by the masses. books, tv, movies, music, film, web sites, newspapers, billboards etc... etc... are all great ways of influencing people.

WHAT IS THE PURPOSE OF WHEELER ANTABANEZ'S ATTACK ON SOCIETY?

my sole purpose is to encourage the people who have taken an interest in what i have said. i want to see more school shootings. i want to hear about churches being burned all across the world. i want all the people who are fed up with the way things have become to make it different. my goal is to rule the world just long enough for me to throw it away.

February 6, 2000

what has happened that today can be so much better than yesterday? i am so bound by circumstance that i cannot escape myself. i am paying my debt to fate insuring my misery on this earth will be whole and complete. the drugs that promised to save me have left me convulsing in the gutter. the women who have loved me have left me shattered and cold and the trust that i once had in myself fluctuates between impotence and omnipotence. who can I be if i'm not really me. the ordinary has passed me by and the only consolation is that my life is anything but boring. it is from this fear of my own mind in which i draw my greatest hope.

February 7, 2000

just a stupid whore

your social life is such a bore

waitress clothes

oiled skin

this is where your life begins

your mothers prize

a pack of lies

soap opera junky

brain of a monkey

retarded

illiterate

bitch

February 8, 2000

I NEED SOME FUCKING MONEY! for those of you who don't know i have not actually worked in many months. my old public relations job was ripped out from under me and i have been left penniless. what i need is some prospects. what i need is a book publisher for my book, but who will publish such a work? everyone seems to be looking for just a little more of the same. the same kind of music the same kind of book the same style clothes, that same comfortable experience so they can get the little ticket that says they're cool (or at least acceptable) really the only person i can blame is myself. it is my laziness that has landed me in the position that i am in. there are thousands of publishers in america and none of them have even seen it. what shall i do? do you know? i am terrible at managing my own affairs. things are going to have to change because my plans are too important to let slip by the wayside. i need help.

February 9, 2000

who to do...what for to do...why for to do...eat fish...yank squirrels...hoist fish....spread goats.

February 10, 2000

who's gonna get it next? so far its been yahoo, zdtv, amazon, etc... do you think you're safe? bill gates won't be able to save you this time. good work guys just stay away from my site.

February 11, 2000

today is a wonderful day. today is a day of waking from dreams and laughing. there is no snooze button on my baby and i am awake very early. i don't mind. when i went to sleep last night my mind was spinning with a million theory's that my dreams have dampered and dulled. pieces of the theory of relativity dance within my head but all the most important lessons that i should have remembered are gone until the next drunken conversation. why could a man like einstein have such clarity when my world seems to be so cloudy. i can think of two reasons off the top of my head. one he actually tried to figure out the world which is a serious commitment that i have never undertaken and the second reason is that he is obviously smarter than me. einstein was able to actually think and comprehend concepts that no matter how many times are explained to me still seem too abstract for a valid place in my reality.

lately i have been thinking about the relationship between smart and stupid and i can't really find a clear definition for either one. stupidity begins where intelligence leaves off, but it all depends on the observer's own intelligence. i look around at the general population with an overwhelming sense of superiority. the reason for this is because while i deal with humans on an individual basis i am automatically measuring what i know to be my own intellectual limitations by how they are acting in my point of reference. usually people turn up stupid compared to me. there is however a large number of people who are indeed smarter than me. they have a higher notch on the intellectual yard stick and look upon me with the same contempt that i thought i owned. so smart and stupid are not clearly defined because there is no point of reference to define intelligence. stay tuned to this page for more on this subject at a later date.

February 12, 2000

"QUALITY FOR SHEEP IS WHAT THE SHEPARD SAYS"

phaedrus-zen & the art of motorcycle mainte-nance

February 13, 2000

and i hope you suffered

in those last moments

and i hope you will suffer

for all eternity

because if you are suffering

then your prayers have been answered

and god is real

February 14, 2000

my breakfast tastes like mud because my taste
buds have turned to sand.

February 15, 2000

STAR-A SELF-LUMINOUS SELF-CONTAINING
MASS OF GAS IN WHICH THE ENERGY GENER-
ATED BY NUCLEAR REACTIONS IN THE INTERI-
OR IS BALANCED BY THE OUTFLOW OF ENERGY
TO THE SURFACE AND IN WHICH INWARD-
DIRECTED GRAVITATIONAL FORCES AND THE
OUTWARD-DIRECTED GAS AND RADIATION
PRESSURES ARE IN BALANCE

February 16, 2000

jimmy hendrix was a nigger

jesus christ and grandma too

brian warner was a nigger

NIGGER

NIGGER

NIGGER

NIGGER

NIGGER

February 17, 2000

Editor,

I have to say that I was appalled to learn that the Internet's bad seeds have sprouted even in our quiet community. One evening at the dinner table my 12-year-old son told me he found a web site devoted to the sanatorium buildings on the Hilltop Property. This peaked my interest so I logged on to the site by going to www.over-brooksanatorium.com.

I looked through the site and even though I found it to be well researched and very informative the writing was incredibly disturbing and peppered with vulgarities. But unfortunately the real problem was much worse than foul language. I noticed that sometimes when I went over the pictures with my mouse, the little pointer would turn into a hand. These turned out to be hidden hyperlinks and when I clicked on them it took me into a whole world of pornography and obscene satanic writings. Just the thought of my son Brian jr. at his impressionable age being subjected to such evil on the web makes me want to throw my computer in the garbage

This letter is a call to action to all the moral, decent, concerned parents in this community that don't want strange people terrorizing their children. The worst part about the situation is that we had our parental controls turned on and since the bad content was hidden this site managed to sneak by unnoticed. The Internet is the most dangerous form of media for children because it reaches them as they sit in the apparent safety of their homes and schools.

This is exactly why we need more laws pertaining to the Internet. Unfortunately our most valuable tool is being exploited and we need to heal that wound before we all lose our heads. If we don't the wrong person is bound to see the true power of it and use it for the ultimate evil.

So let's not let this one slide. This horrible person is located somewhere right in this town just under our noses and I for one am not willing to let my children or yours fall victim. I have always felt safe in this town lets keep it that way.

Sincerely,

Brian Warner

February 18, 2000

up all night having sex. too tired to write.

February 19, 2000

i have been itching for days

the victim of a cursed drug binge

my nails are crusted with blood

the backs of my knees are open and raw

always said i wouldn't go this far

always said i wouldn't do this

but

for now

my prescription is all gone

and its ok to talk about it

doesn't matter if the cops break down the door

my healing can begin

my skin can once again glow

my hair will finally get washed

my wounds will be bandaged and treated

but who knows what tonight will bring

or if there will ever be tomorrow

February 20, 2000

girls love a poet so

FUCK YOU

February 21, 2000

last night i was arrested for taking noise into my
lungs and throwing it out my mouth

February 22, 2000

we are all hooked up to high speed digital drama

in love with information

bound by ones and zeros

seduced by organized energy pulsating inside a plastic package

February 23, 2000

happy birthday zvovz

February 24, 2000

FUCK IT

February 25, 2000

no explanation is needed

because no explanation will do

my words will all whither

my fans will recede

and all that's left will be you

February 26, 2000

man will never precede beast

man is an animal

man will collide with his own nature

civilization will be revealed as a fraud

concrete will turn to dust

roads will become mere trails in the forest

parking lots fields of grass

one day even the plastic will be gone

we are nothing

lives are just a joke on the living

February 27, 2000

the whole world's coming to an end

February 28, 2000

mommy i just wanted you to know that i have benefited from your strain

and my mind has evolved into a machine

February 29, 2000

my bloody tissue looks like a dead mouse in the toilet

March 1, 2000

my teachers were stupid

my parents were frauds

the things that have shaped me were dirty and
wrong

explanations are futile

salvation's a bore

i prefer to spend my time as a whore

you dream of me sober

but i'm not coming back

too many hits and my eyes have turned black

March 2, 2000

HE'S JUST

a victim of the drug culture

incredible tolerance for pain

looks horrible

one step closer to the end than the rest of us

this month is a study in drugs

how much drugs won't kill him

how many nights will this last

you don't know him

he don't even know him

there is nothing left to know

continuing to fight

violent offenses

laughing all the way despite the shame

despite the pain

cocaine

ACTING

never stop and go to work

the proposition of the gun

lonely people should be allowed

death is around every corner

and peeks at him from the shadows

mad dog gatherings

nazi regime

fastidious dress

gone to shit at the seams

March 3, 2000

so much to say but not today

March 4, 2000

Eric's Suicide Note

By now it's over. If you are reading this my mission is complete. I have finished revolutionizing the neoeuphoric infliction of my internal terror. Your children who have ridiculed me, who have chosen not to accept me, who have treated me like I am not worth their time are dead. THEY ARE FUCKING DEAD. Surely you will try to blame it on the clothes I wear, the music I listen to, or the way I choose to present myself—but no. Do not hide behind my choices. You need to face the fact that this comes as a result of YOUR CHOICES. Parents and Teachers, YOU FUCKED UP. You have taught these kids to be gears and sheep. To think and act like those who came before them, to not accept what is different. YOU ARE IN THE WRONG. I may have taken their lives and my own—but it was your doing. Teachers, Parents, LET THIS MASSACRE BE ON YOUR SHOULDERS UNTIL THE DAY YOU DIE. Am I insane? Maybe. Is it my fault? No. I did not choose this life, but I have indeed chosen to exit it. You may think the horror ends with the bullet in my head—but you wouldn't be so lucky. All that I can leave you with to decipher what more extensive death is to come is "12Skizto." You have until April 26th. Goodbye.

Eric Harris, April 19th

March 5, 2000

don't think too much about it

just keep it coming

reality can be ignored

just keep it coming

try not to think

soon it will be over and we can all laugh about it

except you won't be laughing

and i will be dead

March 6, 2000

bloomfield ave

machine gun in every window

confetti in the air

victory

all of you are fanatics

in the making

March 7, 2000

i don't need drugs

March 8, 2000

her saliva is liquid crack

sweet

addictive

tongue in my mouth and in a minute i'll be free

its not what you think

its not what you've heard

ITS BETTER

its everything

March 9, 2000

she thought for a second about jumping, but turned away instead. the laughter from the water thirty feet below resounded off the sheer face of the granite cliff and echoed around the swimming hole.

this is how we met.

as i climbed the last turn of the steep mountain path that led to the top of the cliff, i got my first glimpse of her. she was bathed in late afternoon sunlight that caught her auburn hair and set it ablaze. her form captivated me, its intricate curves perfectly framed in her tight white bikini. i paused for a minute catching my breath after the steep climb and wiped the sweat off my brow with the back of my arm.

again i heard the distant laughter from her friends below and i noticed a troubled look on her face. i walked beside her and stood at the edge of the cliff. peering over, I felt the utter intoxication of vertigo pulling me towards the cool water below. but this beautiful young woman standing next to me, looking so sad, compelled me to remain on the rocky ledge.

"do you want to jump first?" i asked.

she looked into my eyes for the first time. "no you go ahead." she replied coldly.

she stared me straight in the eyes and her gaze captured me.

"it's too hot to climb back down the trail," i said, "if you jump the water will catch you."

her eyes began to laugh and the last thing i saw was her mouth turn into a smile as i fell into a perfect double back flip into the sweet refresh-ment of the cool pennsylvanian quarry. i sur-faced to a round of applause for my perfect dive and as i rubbed the water from my eyes i turned back to the cliff. she was standing silhouetted in the sun. every curve was tensed in perfection and her shocking beauty forced my admiring spectators into the background. for that moment all that existed was the cool water lapping at my body and her shadow burned into the sky.

then she took flight. she spread her arms as if they were wings and flew fearlessly into the water below.

thirty feet of sky and the water caught her just as i had promised.

thirty feet of sky and life will never be the same.

March 10, 2000

if i had the funding i'd kill you all

plant a bomb in every mall

March 11, 2000

i can't remember exactly what happened last night but i woke up this morning with a swastika tattoo and a canteen full of blood

March 12, 2000

last night my golden retriever Rusty was hit by a car and broke both of his hind legs. he was obviously hurt too bad to be saved so i blew his head off with my shotgun. i haven't slept and i am covered in mud from burying his body in my backyard. this is the saddest day of my life.

March 13, 2000

the real evil in america today is the media

none of your minds are safe

March 14, 2000

couldjya help an old alter boy father

March 15, 2000

everyone will remember

and then they will forget

March 16, 2000

everyone below hitler was a sheep

A FUCKING SHEEP

quality for sheep is what the shepherd says

fascism is only cool if you're the fuehrer

you are all mindless little sheep

and i hate you for it

when i am shepherd you will all learn a better
way

March 17, 2000

Wheeler Antabanez = Matt Kent

if any of you little primates had bothered to read my book you would have already known this.

lately i have been barraged by e-mail's (and phone calls) from a bunch of 13 year old kids.

it seems they some how figured out my real identity and have nothing better to do than bother me.

this is as it should be.

Fame = Annoying Fans

these children are idiots.

most of the e-mail's i receive from these kids read as if they were written by monkeys.

they never have anything new to say

they are never funny

in fact

they are so monotonous and boring that i don't even bother to read them anymore.

so what do they do when i ignore them?

they call my house.

yeah my name is in the phone book

all you have to do is dial 411.

but why would you?

i have no desire to speak with you

and i have absolutely no patience for children.

so lets get things nice and sparkling clear:

i have no interest in finding you.

i have no interest in meeting you.

i don't care about your stupid problems.

if i saw you dying in the street i would just keep
walking.

March 18, 2000

all my emotions have died

the only thing i have left inside of me is confidence

soon the whole world will be at my mercy

things can only get worse from here

March 19, 2000

how can a world of people around me mean so little

aren't there any cool people on this planet

March 20, 2000

twas the month before columbine and all through the town all the children were living and laughing like clowns

4/20

March 21, 2000

I AM WEE TODD DID

I AM SOFA KING WEE TODD DID

March 22, 2000

woke up this morning in a rage

destroying the things i love

destroying myself

smashing everything i thought i needed just to
see if i really need it

snap decisions

a slip of the tongue

the whip on my legs

my fist in my face

my hammer in my teeth

still can't forgive

certainly can't forget

won't let myself

my mind will not grant me a reprieve

even sleep won't bring me to a better place

only the big sleep will

the one true rest

but no rest today

and no rest from last night

so what to do?

kill myself because i woke up on the wrong side of the bed?

No

i have made it through too many tragedies for that

i will just suffer

i will be the mammal that i am and feel what i feel

i will get high

i will get drunk

i will punch my walls until something breaks

i will smash myself with the stick i keep in the corner

i will cut long gashes into my legs

i will feel better

i always do

March 23, 2000

these dreams are killing me

March 24, 2000

it would be nice to climb a tree with a book on a nice fall day. i picture the tree to be ripened by autumn into a million shades of golden stars. people would never look up to see the strange, tattooed boy reading in the tree. they would pass without noticing and in turn go unnoticed. people go by unnoticed so often. they just mesh together like the cinderblocks in your basement. each block is just as important as the next, but they are all the same and they all basically perform the same function equally well. the real question is not how important the cinderblock is but how important is the house? the answer: not very important at all (unless it's your house). who wouldn't sell their soul for humanity, but in turn hates most of the people that surround them.

March 25, 2000

last night i had a very strange dream. i was standing in the middle of a huge steel pen that was packed tight with hundreds and hundreds of cattle. surrounding me was a heavy duty metal frame that acted as a sort of shark cage and kept me safe. in this cage with me there was a small calf who looked to be only a few days old. the calf was bound and tied so that it couldn't move and was forced to just stand there in the middle of the cage.

the only other things besides me and the cow was a large framing hammer and a butcher knife that were sitting in the corner. as soon as i noticed these items i set to work on the baby calf. i took the hammer to its back and started smashing its tiny little rib cage one rib at a time. i beat the cow mercilessly and at the sounds of its screams the cattle outside of our cage began to react violently.

simultaneously they began to stampede, but there was nowhere to go. they tried to smash through my metal cage to save the baby and they tried to break free of their pen but they were hopelessly trapped. soon the air was thick with dust and the screams of pain were coming from all the animals. in their rage and their panic they couldn't help but collide and trample each other to death.

my cage kept me safe and in the end my little calf and i were the only ones left alive. the cattle lay dead by the hundreds forming an impossible sea of gory flesh.

the calf wasn't doing so well and could no longer stand on it's own accord so i decided to end it. i walked over to the corner and grabbed the butcher knife. gently i tilted it's head back and slit it's soft little throat. blood ran hot over my hand and when i woke i could still feel it flowing in rivulets over my outstretched arm.

March 26, 2000

FUCK YOU I HATE YOU

March 27, 2000

like hitler to a jew i'm in love with you

March 28, 2000

$ometimes things are hard

right now turmoil is my companion

to be poor in a world of riches is unacceptable

so i will persist

i will prevail

all the odds tell me that i will fail

but i will not

i will win

March 29, 2000

i have jesus power

i have jesus

jesus is bleeding on my rug

i have been raping and beating him all night

March 30, 2000

my face is contaminated with frowns

my smiles have moved on

not you but me

not us but me

i can't relax

i can't stand still

i want to die

i want to live

i want

i want

i want

i want

March 31, 2000

yesterday i smashed my head so hard that i crumpled to the ground and fell asleep like a little baby.

when i woke i was in a magickal world filled with birds and fairies

.mike patton was playing the harpsichord at my feet.

am i dead?

April 1, 2000

now the sun's a hot star

and mercury's hot too

venus is the brightest planet

earth's home to me and you

mars is the red one

jupiter's most wide

saturn's got those icy rings

and uranus spins on it's side

neptune's really windy

and pluto's really small

well we wanted to name the planets and now
we've named them all

bc

April 2, 2000

i looked up and saw the road

i became aware that i was upside down

i tried to change my position

but my limbs were gripped tight by jagged
metal

my face was crystallized with blood and glass

a tear ran up my forehead

silence inside me

only the beeping of the keys

April 3, 2000

my mind is being nibbled by a thousand
maggots

they crept in through the gash on my head

i need some bug spray

April 4, 2000

"The present drug laws are a pathetic mess. The old adage that ignorance of the law is no excuse becomes a ludicrous statement when the laws themselves are rooted in ignorance. One classical example of this is the classification of the stimulant Cocaine as a narcotic. One is reminded of the King in Alice in Wonderland who made up his own language as he went along with total disregard for the accepted definitions of words. I will not even go into the question of whether any law enforcement agency has the moral or Constitutional right to dictate what substances we may or may not take into our own adult bodies. Any modern individual whose mind is not immersed in the slavish dung pit of Dark Age unreasoning knows that reliable education—not criminal penalization—is the answer to whatever drug problems exist. Nevertheless, we must contend realistically with the powers that unfortunately be at this time. They are the ones with the badges, guns, gavels and goons. "

Adam Gottlieb

April 5, 2000

reality is keeping me sad

every time life gets good

my happiness blooms and promptly sours

maybe its because the drugs are all gone

maybe its because the money is all gone

i am left with little choice

a life of crime is the only way

the world has turned on me

and now its my turn to inflict the pain

get ready

i'm going to need your help

April 6, 2000

women have always been a mystery to me

why should anything be different today

confusion and pain

unresolved conversations leave me empty when
i should feel full

silence the only answer to my questions

i am coming undone

no mercy

no forgiveness

no reprieve

no justice and no comfort in my emotions

what have i done

have i thrown it all away

have i said too much or maybe too little

is this about to end or has it just begun

?

April 7, 2000

Subj: Check out april flowers coax may showers
Date: 4/6/00 10:05:01 AM Eastern Daylight Time
From: Justaresident@aol.com
To: deadman@welcometohell.net

We have read the last two days and your are really feeling sorry for your self. Stop and think of what you have done to the others in you life. It's time too get you ass in high gear and start you life. Really who do you think you are the only victim in the world its time your writings are all about you what a bout the rest of the world. Come on lets get going. We will look to see change for the better in your daily diary.

my reply:

Subj: (a valuable lesson and a retort to your accusations)
Date: 4/6/00 10:53:10 AM Eastern Daylight Time
From: deadman@welcometohell.net
To: Justaresident@aol.com

you are a fucking idiot

you understand nothing

regurgitating guilty sayings that have been passed down from mommy

i don't feel sorry for myself and i don't feel sorry for you

when you die you will have done nothing

no one will remember

when i die it will shake the foundations of the world

i have something to say and all you can do is judge and twist my words

fuck you

keep your opinions to yourself

no one is listening to you

no one cares what you have to say

but they listen to me

and they do what i say

and one day so will you

you are a purposeless sheep

speaking a sheep language

in a world of hopeless sheep

i have transcended god

don't bother to reply as all your e-mails have
been blocked

and my interest has depleted with every word i
have written

(a valuable lesson and a retort to your accusations)

April 8, 2000

this is one line describing itself as containing no
information

April 9, 2000

yesterday i took my cat (photon) to the vet and he told me that she was pregnant

i had to shell out $350.00 for an abortion but as it turns out it was worth it

photon was bleeding a lot after the operation (she was pretty far into the pregnancy) and the vet gave her some painkillers which i decided to take myself

i have done my share of pills but never in my life have i tasted such a potent narcotic

i took one dose early last night and my mind is still reeling

the little green pill took me into a world of pleasure that made heroin look like a mild rush

i have thirty more of these pills and even though the cats in pain i'm gonna keep them for myself

when i run out i'm gonna have to get the cat pregnant again so i can get some more

i love drugs

April 10, 2000

we are all alone

has that sunk in yet?

if not it will

all your life you will watch people drift past you
and turn into memories

you will trust and you will be wrong

you will be:

crushed

beaten

and abandoned

your heart will turn:

cold, callused and dead

and then you will do it again

and then it will happen again

and if you live through that one you'll do it again

why?

we are mammals

we are men and women and we need each other

but no matter what the circumstance

we are always alone

and we always will be

April 11, 2000

fragments of fantasy

colors of youth

yearning and longing only for truth

teenage america tragic and screwed

turning and tangled if only for food

to feed their illusions

to quench all their fears

to break out of eggshells they've been trapped
in for years

shaped by the masses

gelled by the norm

running and crashing away from the storm

beating and cursing this sea of regret

wishing somehow I'd finally forget

how did this happen

what have you done

wishing i could put out the sun

and kill all the masses

and laugh as it passes

slash all the flowers

burn all the trees

thrashing

destroying

all of my needs

April 12, 2000

i feel good

i think my plan just might work

8 more days to columbine

April 13, 2000

today i killed a fisherman and i stole his pole

today i killed a fisherman he ain't never gonna
grow old

i laughed in his face and put him in place

now i walk river road and i step on a toad

i'll use his pole for my own type of goal

i don't need it for dinner

i need to get thinner

i just want to catch a big fish and kill it

April 14, 2000

Subj: hello wheeler
Date: 4/13/00 9:07:14 PM Eastern Daylight Time
From: Sherockstar@aol.com
To: deadman@welcometohell.net,

"Ode to Wheeler and the Asylum"
by lindsey

Half torn bricks beckon to me

I can hear their cries of shame.

They call to me from confined rooms.

Drugs keep them insane.

I follow where their voices lead, up and down
the paths.

They call to me.

They tell me "breathe."

So I breathe a breath of death.

My lungs inflate.

As theirs once did,

with a tortured sense of grief

154

I want to share their lives,

their lives sadly brief.

April 15, 2000

"you're dragging me through the mud baby

I need you like a dog needs RABIES

I wish I could count on you to be there

but you're just a fountain of maybes..."

JCPENNEY?

April 16, 2000

KILL YOUR PARENTS

April 17, 2000

how many more days do you think you have to live?

3 more days?

as far as i'm concerned you're already dead

April 18, 2000

everybody's so full of shit

April 19, 2000

what's wrong kids

does everyone around you seem like a fucking asshole

have you tried to fit in all your life and failed

here's my advice

if you can't join them

fight them

grab your daddy's shotgun and teach the world a lesson

show them what the world would be like without you

show them what they deserve to see

show them that they cannot change you

and that they will die trying

4/20

April 20, 2000

this will be my last entry and the end of welcometohell

last night i got arrested because of the things i said on my web site

my bail was set at $50,000 and my parents have just bailed me out

i make no apologies for the things that i said and i want you all to know that i take my writing very seriously.

now that i have been turned loose into the world and everyone knows me i feel a new relief

i feel purged of my anger (at least for the moment) and i am ready to show you all another side of me

wheeler antabanez is dead forever

matt kent can be a loving person as well as a ruthless hate machine

everything that i have written was a cleansing of myself and i have no regrets

there will be no further changes to welcometohell except for a link to my new web site which will be coming soon

matt kent

i make this stand and i have always made this stand for the good of all of us

if there was ever a sin, that sin is censorship

censorship implies that you as an individual are not capable of making your own choices

censorship and your tolerance of it is what turns humans into sheep

we all make our own choices and i have decided to take my daily journal and my book off the web

i do this to keep myself out of jail and for no other reason

if you never got a chance to read what i have written never fear

soon my book "gasstationthoughts" will be published and available in bookstores across the country (as soon as i find a publisher)

as an appendix to my book all three months worth of my journal entries will be included

now that i have succeeded with my plan and have become a famous Internet rock star i feel it is time to move towards bigger and better things

my calling has always been towards the silver screen

currently i am working on my first novel which will be accompanied by a full length motion picture

i will leave you kids for now with one piece of parting advice

this world will try with all its infinite power to change the person that you are

someone or some group of people will always be in disagreement with your own personal philosophies

NEVER LET THEM CHANGE YOU

you were created to be what you are and what you are is beautiful

thank you to all my fans

thank you to all that love me

now is the time when i will need you the most

until i speak again...

matt kent